THE BEST
Tree House
EVER

How to Build a Backyard Tree House
the Whole World Will Talk About

Maurice Barkley

Skyhorse Publishing

The world is so full
of a number of things,
I'm sure we should all
be as happy as kings.
　　—Robert Louis Stevenson

Contents

Preface

I remember the approach of my sixty-fifth birthday and my pending retirement. Both events evoked mixed emotions. That time of life works well for some and not so well for others, regardless of the plans that they made.

I thought about it from time to time, but retirement arrived in the same boat that had delivered my high school graduation day. On that happy day long ago, I gave no thought to the fact that my life as a dependent child was nearing its end. Another major part was about to begin, for better or worse.

Fortunately, it has worked out quite well, but it has taken many years of experience and many evenings of quiet reflection to appreciate my good fortune and my good luck. This book begins shortly after my retirement. Among other things, it is a good example of unintended consequences in the pursuit of rainbows. As a child recently told me, "You did good, Mister."

Introduction

I think that I shall never see
a poem lovely as a tree.

I was a very young man when I first heard this song by Fred Waring and the Pennsylvanians. It is still among my favorites. There is magic when you are up in the arms of a tree. Secret places—things that can't quite be seen. Listening to the whispering as the leaves play with the passing breeze. Sitting below a leaf and watching it glow as the sun shines on top.

I call the picture above "Genesis." It shows the joy on the faces of my daughter's children after I built a simple platform in a maple tree out back. This was where it all started several years ago. Soon they asked for a rope bridge going to the next tree. I was reluctant, but I did it because that's what grandpas do. At some time during the construction I discovered that it was a lot of fun, so I kept going and only looked back to admire my work.

Now, several years later, I have in my yard six tree houses linked by seven bridges and a small deck suspended between two locust trees.

There are four seasons where my wife and I live. For half the year I build and play outside. When cold weather arrives, you can find me in my basement workshop building a new tree house or maybe a device with a crank and pulleys to lift small things from the ground.

But the best thing from these experiences, the very best thing, has been the children. Imagine watching a five-year-old climb into my trees for the first time. To see their wide smiles and shining eyes is pay back with interest for all my work.

We have a guest book. We ask anyone who climbs the tree to sign their name and city of origin. They all sign and heap praise on the builder. To date we have most states and about fifteen countries.

A Short, Sweet Story

Once upon a time a young lady with a camcorder came to visit. She went through the entire tree complex filming and providing her own commentary on what she saw. Later, in our house where several people were visiting, she turned on her camcorder, pointed it at my wife, and said, "This is the wife of THE MAKER." She then turned to focus on me and said, "and this is THE MAKER."

Well . . . Well, well. Are you curious? If so, follow the yellow brick road and enter THE ABODE OF THE MAKER.

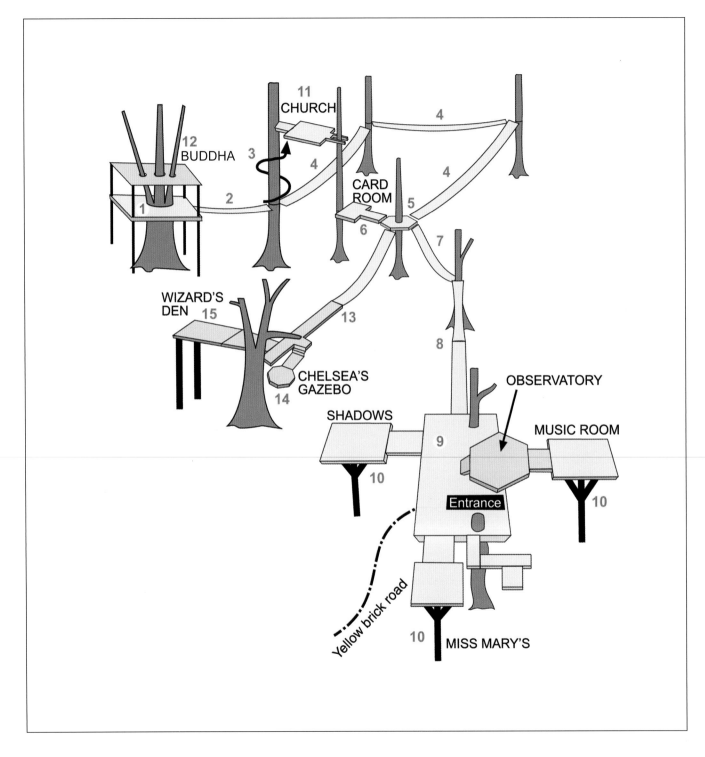

Tour

It all began here—a simple platform with a tree in the middle **1**. A solid-and-rope bridge **2** to a nearby pine was next. While there, I made my first attempt at a spiral staircase **3**. It was not good and soon removed. Three more bridges **4** brought me to a maple tree, where I built a transfer platform **5**, a short walkway, and a small platform hung between the maple and a nearby pine **6**. The platform was finished with railings all around and a tent cloth roof. Another rope bridge reached the last maple in the backyard **7**. From there it took a combination of a rope and solid bridge to reach two locust trees **8** where I built a floating deck **9,** and then I attached three lollypop houses to it. **10** That done, I returned to the big pine tree and built a proper spiral staircase. At the top I made a platform hung between the two pines **11**. The following spring a tiny church found a home up there in the pines. Needing a new project, I returned to the original platform, reinforced it a bit, and then built a second story with little steps going up and a narrow walkway going back to another curious little house **12**. My latest effort was another double bridge **13** with Chelsea's Gazebo **14** and The Wizard's Den **15** at its end.

This view from the driveway is the first sight that greets our visitors.

Day by day the view from this spot constantly changes. On certain wonderful, sunny days I find myself wishing that things could stay just as they were at that moment. My trees forever green. My wife's flowers forever in blossom. Our grandchildren forever young. This is my answer to that wish.

Once here, all you must do is FOLLOW THE YELLOW BRICK ROAD.

From the flower-covered arbor you will find a winding path made with real yellow bricks.

The road leads to this ladder. There is nowhere to go but up.

I stand here to watch the faces of small children when, for the first time, they climb up to a new world where they can walk through the middle of a tree, watching the small leaves of the locust tree forever move and dance in the sun and shadow; where tiny doors on tiny houses are just the right size; where wind chimes play my theme song.

First you climb the ladder, then you climb the stair steps. At the top, you find yourself on a wooden deck high up in the air where the leaves of the locust trees form a cavern that shuts out the rest of the world. Perhaps you are alone, free to go in any direction. The little place with the blue door is called Miss Mary's Teahouse. Miss Mary (in residence in the small photo above) is my one and only granddaughter, so the first house belongs to her. It has a Dutch door, screened windows, a table, six benches, electric lights, and other mysterious objects. To the left are steps leading to Victoria's Tearoom and the wishing wheel. Near right is a crank device that can lift a tray of jasmine tea and sugar cookies from below.

To the left of Miss Mary's Teahouse is Victoria's Tearoom.

Left to right in the image are Sarah and Victoria drinking blue air tea and discussing secrets. Further on down the walkway to the left is the wishing wheel.

Here is a gathering place called The Observatory.

One of my favorite places is this open, five-sided structure. It was originally built to hold an astronomical telescope. Hey, if you are up in a tree, you are that much closer to the moon, planets, and stars. Right? Sadly, I discovered that even during a calm evening with no trace of a breeze, everything wiggles constantly. We now use it for other things like lunch. Often I go there after dark when the colored lamps are lit and the mosquitoes don't realize that there is a victim up in the middle of the tree. My coffee just tastes better there.

A little left again shows the bridge to the Other Place.

Here we have two explorers. One goes to the observatory to hunt for traces of the missing telescope and one cranks the snack elevator, which is used primarily to transport juice boxes, chips, hot dogs, and the like. There is a better view of the elevator in the small picture at top left. My coffee chair can be seen just to the right of the pink sweater. Between the explorers, the solid part of the bridge leads to a rope and plank bridge, which in turn melts into a wall of leaves in the distance.

More to the left, as seen from the Observatory, is the house called "Shadows."

The path to the Other Place.

A small visitor named this "Bridge to the Other Place" quite some time ago. When she reached the end of the rope bridge she ducked under the leaves, looked ahead, then turned and called to her companions, "There's a whole other place over here."

The Card Room

The first stop at the Other Place is called the Card Room, but it also serves as a lunchroom, meeting room, tearoom, or whatever you wish it to be. Later I built another snack elevator on the walkway.

A more recent picture of the Card Room sporting a new roof.

My snack elevator is holding up rather well. It is a simpler design consisting of a single rope going over a large overhead wheel and down to a wicker basket usually filled with some of the many pine cones found in this area.

The Spiral Staircase.

The spiral staircase starts at a height of ten feet and goes on up. As you might imagine, this was a major project. My first attempt was a sad affair, but the second time I got it right. It is a very strong and solid structure.

Finally, the top—my Church in the Pines.

There are things a person remembers from childhood. Snapshots kept in your memory of ordinary events as well as the significant.

I have a memory of a long ago snowfall with tall, soft lumps piled on the big, long needle pine next door. On bitter cold nights those snowy lumps twinkled with bits of reflected starlight. Pure magic. It was there that I imagined my first Church in the Pines.

The Church is suspended between two pine trees. Notice that the tree on the left with the staircase is much thicker and taller than the other.

This is the first bridge that I built; at the beginning of its sixth year, I took it down and rebuilt it with new ropes. I set a maximum of five years for my rebuilding schedule.

The Genesis Tower.

This two-story platform is the last stop on this branch line. The tree also hosts a very big swing, one end of a zip-line, and a ladder to the ground.

A temple called Buddha.

The Best Swing Ever.

A really good swing must have a long rope anchored really high on a limb.

Just a song at twilight.

On most summer days you will find people in this picture, but once in a melancholy while I find myself alone and wishing there were someone with me to share what I see.

How did you do that?

In the following sections I will try to answer the many people, young and old, who have asked that question.

Bridges

- No single cable, rope, screw, bolt, or piece of lumber should provide total support in most applications.
- A safe, secure rope and plank bridge must be built to carry a load far in excess of the expected maximum.
- The anchors or bridge ends should be perpendicular to the line of the bridge to prevent side-to-side sagging.
- The bridge should sag in the middle to allow for the movement of the tree during high winds and to reduce strain when under load.
- All lumber should have a treated exterior and be relatively knot free.
- Screws are better than nails.
- The ideal length of my bridges is ten feet. Fifteen feet is workable, but beyond that requires the use of very strong and expensive material.

My design is shown below.

How high off the ground? If I have a choice, ten to twelve feet, which is high enough to be just a tad scary. How wide? 16-inch planks. (Six planks cut from an 8-foot piece.)

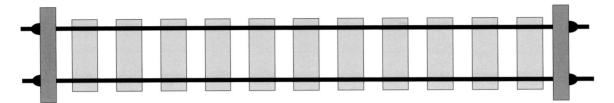

NOTE: A tug of about two inches at either end will pull this rope taut.

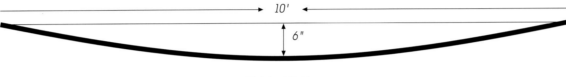

Finished Bridge

My bridge design.

The bridge is made with eight vinyl ropes (244 lb test). There are double hand ropes and double ropes woven between the foot planks. Smaller 1/4-inch vertical ropes are added between each plank

Loop small vertical ropes around large plank ropes. Take up most, but not all, slack.

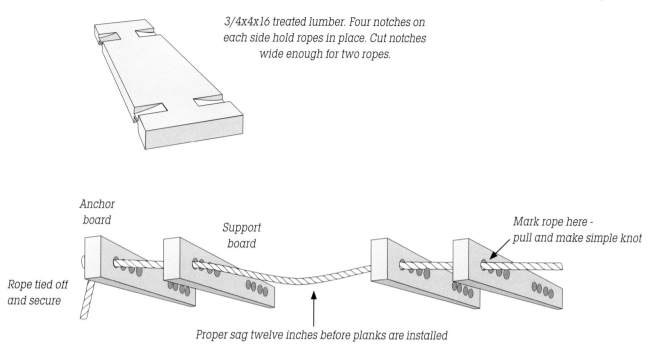

3/4x4x16 treated lumber. Four notches on each side hold ropes in place. Cut notches wide enough for two ropes.

Anchor board

Support board

Mark rope here - pull and make simple knot

Rope tied off and secure

Proper sag twelve inches before planks are installed

You may do this if the eyebolt is very strong:

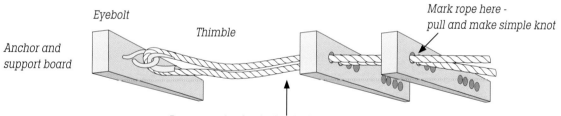

Eyebolt

Thimble

Mark rope here - pull and make simple knot

Anchor and support board

Proper sag twelve inches before planks are installed

Installing the Planks (Side View)

Lay first plank in center of bridge.

Lay next plank as shown and push together. Gap should be about one inch.

Install plank 3 on the other side.

From this point on you may install two or three planks on one side, then keep on alternating sides until all of the planks are in place.

If necessary cut last plank wider or narrower to allow four inches space as shown.

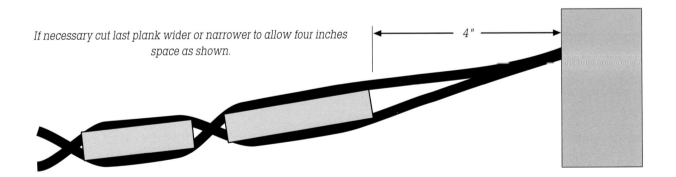

Note that one rope enters the support hole at a sharper angle than the other. To fix this, bolt two thin strips of hardwood as shown below. Snug—not tight.

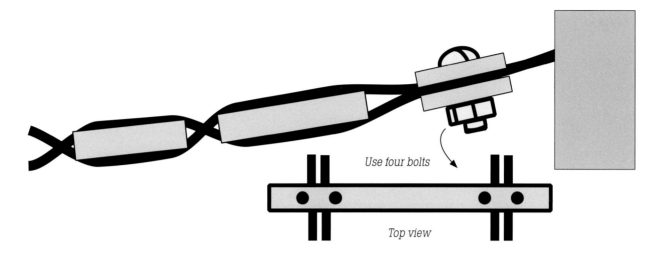

Use four bolts

Top view

Install the vertical ropes and you are finished.

Bridge Anchors

A bridge may be going from tree house to tree house, from tree house to tree, or from tree to tree.

Most bridges coming from a tree house can be anchored to the frame of the tree house. When anchored to a tree, a special frame is required. The following shows my solutions to this problem.

My basic platform provides support for the bridge and bridge users. It also stays level using a design that locks it to the tree trunk as weight is applied to the structure.

This illustration shows the anchor for a single bridge. It provides good balance as the bridge pulls on the center of the tree.

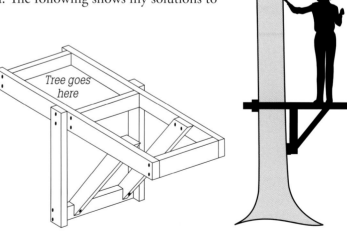

Tree goes here

Basic frame

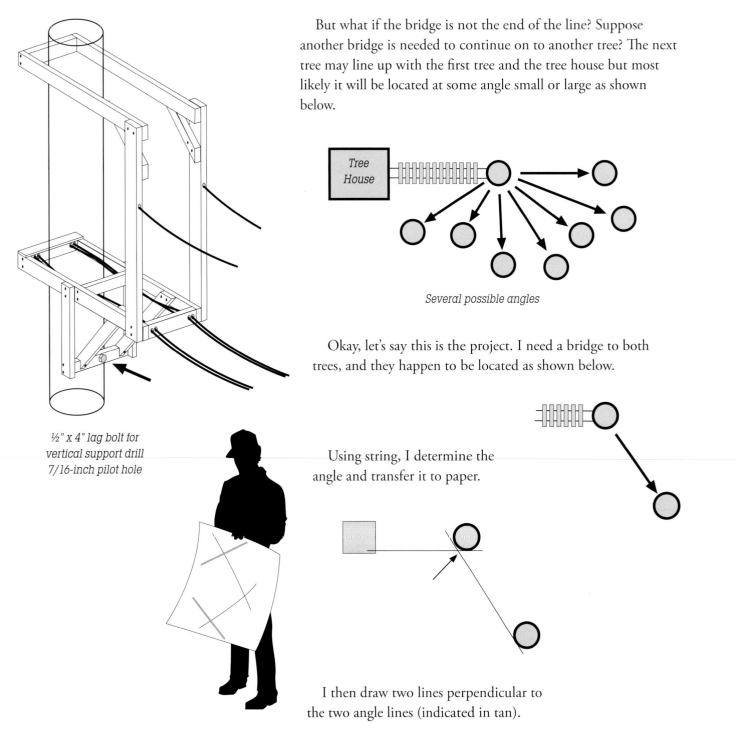

But what if the bridge is not the end of the line? Suppose another bridge is needed to continue on to another tree? The next tree may line up with the first tree and the tree house but most likely it will be located at some angle small or large as shown below.

Several possible angles

Okay, let's say this is the project. I need a bridge to both trees, and they happen to be located as shown below.

½" x 4" lag bolt for vertical support drill 7/16-inch pilot hole

Using string, I determine the angle and transfer it to paper.

I then draw two lines perpendicular to the two angle lines (indicated in tan).

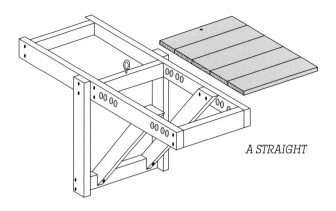

A STRAIGHT

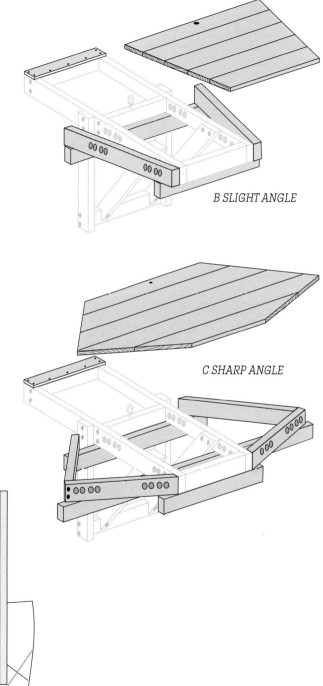

B SLIGHT ANGLE

C SHARP ANGLE

Depending on the angle, I need one of the platforms shown on the right.

Start with a basic frame. The ideal width is sixteen inches—the width of the bridge planks. The other important dimension is the space allowed for the tree trunk. This should be 1/2-inch larger than the trunk diameter to allow for tree growth. If necessary I will shim to reduce the space or increase the all-over width to increase the space.

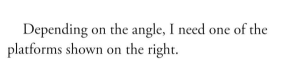

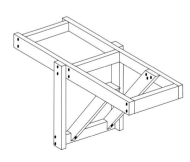

SHIM IF NEEDED

Build the basic frame from treated, knot-free 2x4s, and place it over the paper with the angle. The red perpendicular lines indicate the correct placement of the bridge anchors.

By extending the tan lines you can determine the type of frame you need and the length of the supports.

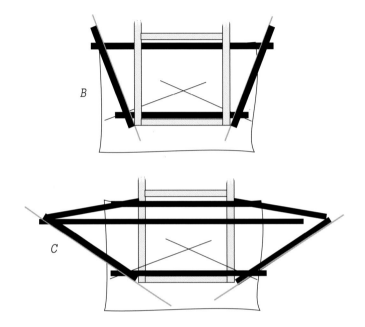

Below are diagrams for proper roping. Notice that the ropes extend through each side and will tend to pull the sides of the base together under load. There will be some side-to-side movement of bases A and B when there is a load on either bridge. This movement will be less than two inches if the bridges are hung properly. If the movement bothers me, it can be controlled by cables as shown below.

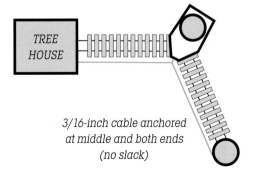

3/16-inch cable anchored
at middle and both ends
(no slack)

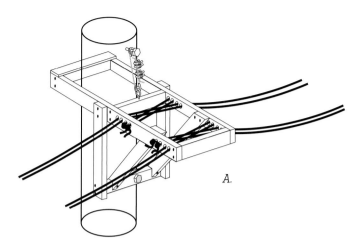

A.

If you wish, you may add extra cable support.

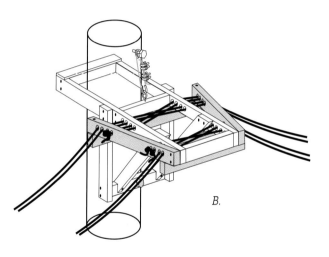

B.

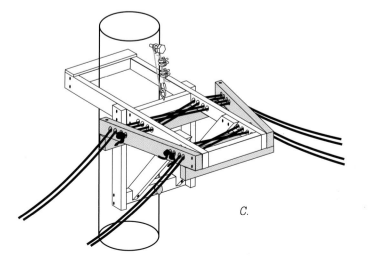

C.

A Word about Rope

When a rope is passed over or through any object, I make sure there are no sharp edges. Even a 2x4 can cause a problem if the rope constantly impacts an edge.

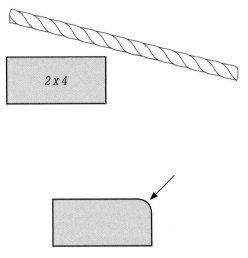

Round the edge with a wood file.

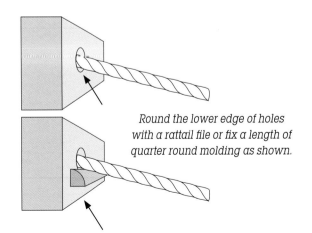

Round the lower edge of holes with a rattail file or fix a length of quarter round molding as shown.

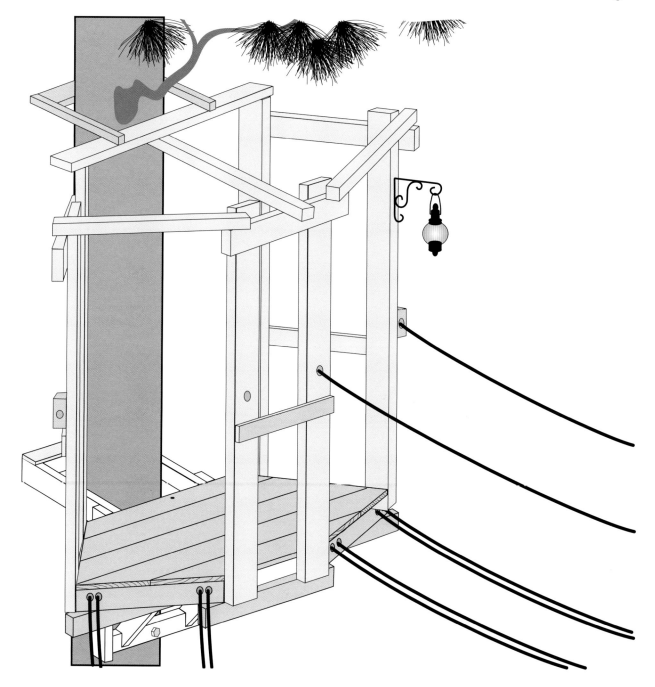

This is a finished installation ready for decoration. Keep in mind that this is only one of many configurations depending on the tree.

Multi-Bridge Transfers

Here is another of many solutions for a two- or multi-bridge transfer. I used a similar configuration at the base of my spiral staircase, because two bridges came in at the bottom.

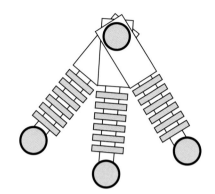

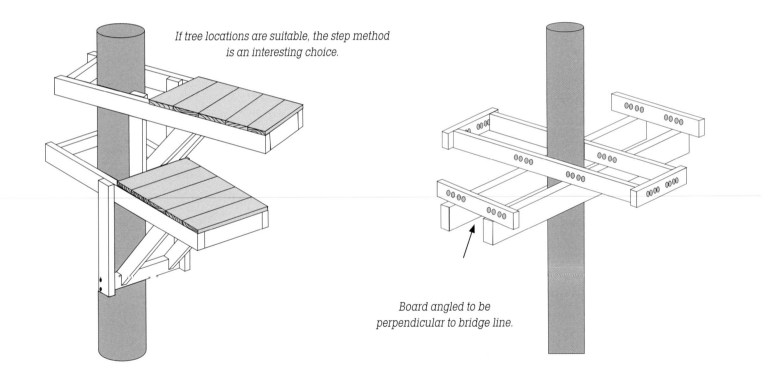

If tree locations are suitable, the step method is an interesting choice.

Board angled to be perpendicular to bridge line.

If there are three or four bridges going to a single tree, I may build a platform that can be left as a simple, open transfer point or enclosed as a tree house.

Another word about stability. Any platform with a tree through its middle must be supported vertically and horizontally.

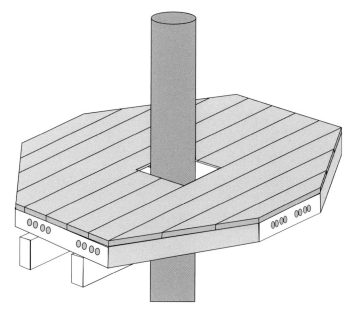

Use standard 1-inch deck lumber for floor. Apply as shown for maximum strength.

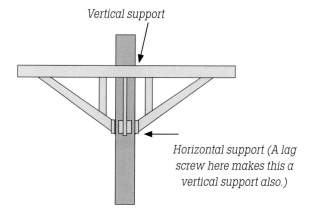

Vertical support

Horizontal support (A lag screw here makes this a vertical support also.)

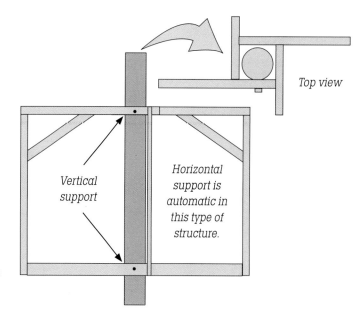

Top view

Vertical support

Horizontal support is automatic in this type of structure.

Another fun solution, if the trees are fairly close, is to make a solid bridge. I use two methods to allow for tree trunk movement. The first is to make a lip on one structure and a solid anchor on the other. The bridge rests on the lip and slides a bit in the wind.

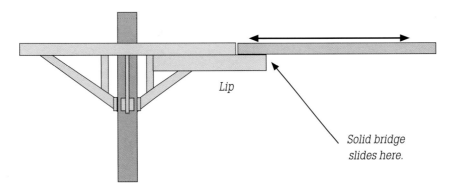

Lip

*Solid bridge
slides here.*

The second method is to support one end loosely with cables.

In this illustration, bridge and platform are one piece.

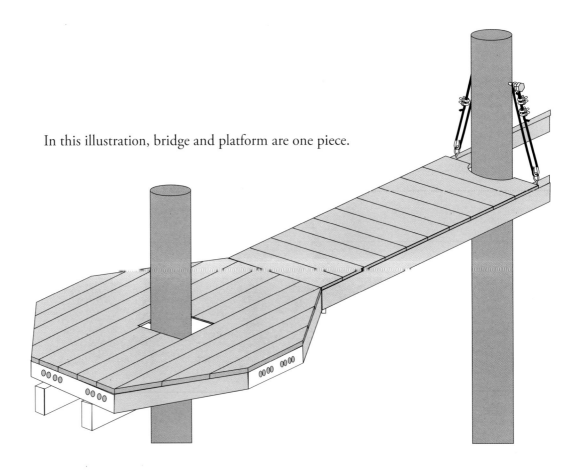

Proper Support

Now is a good time to discuss how to properly support the bridges and platforms just covered.

I use aircraft cable, which is available just about everywhere. It is rust-free and there is no give. The sizes I use are as follows:

3/16" = 850 lb load
1/4" = 1,400 lb load

A cable can be secured with cable clamps or turnbuckles rated to match the cable load. It can be fixed to a tree by a lag screw in the trunk or by looping it over a sturdy limb. Shown below are two methods of securing the cable to the load.

This is one way to support a bridge using a lip. I used this about twelve feet up the tree, where trunk movement is minimal.

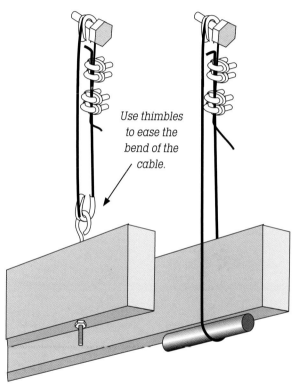

Use thimbles to ease the bend of the cable.

Iron pipe eases bend of cable and distributes load on beam.

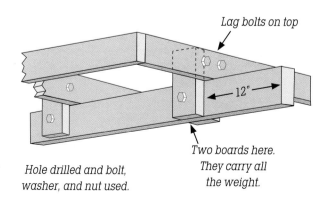

Lag bolts on top

← 12" →

Two boards here. They carry all the weight.

Hole drilled and bolt, washer, and nut used.

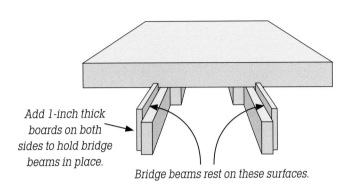

Add 1-inch thick boards on both sides to hold bridge beams in place.

Bridge beams rest on these surfaces.

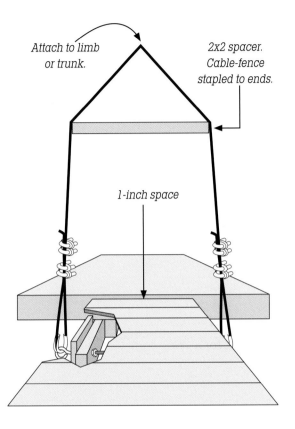

Attach to limb or trunk.

2x2 spacer. Cable-fence stapled to ends.

1-inch space

Ladders and Stairs

Ladders begin the adventure. I use them for all entrances to the trees. Since they are moveable objects, they need to be somewhat heavy so that they stay put. The ladders are a bit difficult for a very young person to climb, but this is deliberate. My entrance ladders are six to seven feet high. A parent can stand there as the child climbs and assist as necessary.

Once the child completes the climb and is up in the trees, he or she has a sense of accomplishment and separation from the ground below. They made it to a magic place on their own.

All 2x4s →

All ¾x6 ←

All 1x6 →

Because I like different levels I use both of these stairs in the trees. Most are small—only two to four steps. They are very sturdy and add interest wherever they appear. All ladders from the ground should be removable to provide security when the owner is not around.

The Spiral Staircase

The entire structure fits like a loose sleeve around the smooth trunk of a tall pine tree. It is hung by an 850-lb test aircraft cable at nine places. The cable is slung under a riser and over a limb or limb stub. I have had 800 pounds of people on the bridge and it has never budged.

My staircase has twelve steps, which is one and a half turns around the trunk. Each riser, or step, is eight inches high, thus lifting the traveler another eight inches up into the trees. The structure is fifty-three inches in diameter as measured through the 12-inch diameter trunk. This leaves a step width of about twenty inches. Head height is about fifty-six inches. If you are taller, bend a little.

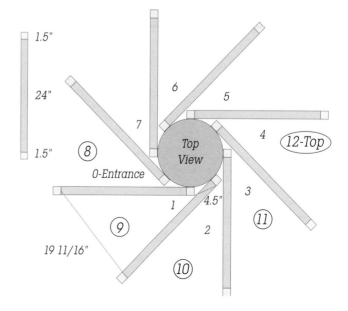

I chose pattern A over pattern B, because by using Pattern A I am able to lock the risers together to make the structure more solid and rigid.

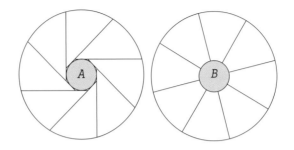

The drawing below shows how the risers are tied together with deck screws. The screws are indicated by red lines.

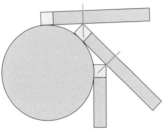

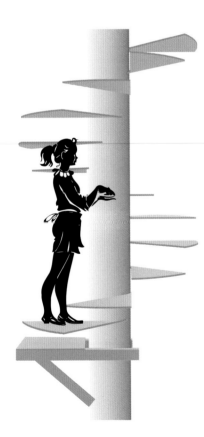

At this point I felt confident enough to go to the lumber store for material. I returned with sixteen 2x2x8s, three 2x8x8s (for the risers), several ¾x4x8s (for the step floors), a few 2x4x8s, some lattice pieces, and an assortment of deck screws. I had some cable and clamps in inventory. The lumber was piled under the tree, my tools gathered, and I went to work.

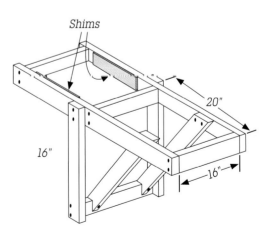

A brace and bridge anchor was first. It was sixteen inches wide and shimmed for the 12-inch trunk. The front stuck out at least twenty inches, as did the steps. When complete, I took off the back board and fitted the unit to the tree. It required a little shimming to get it level, which is very important because the first riser rests on it.

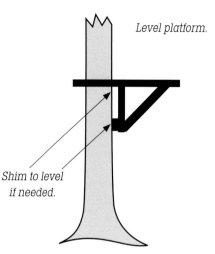

Level platform.

*Shim to level
if needed.*

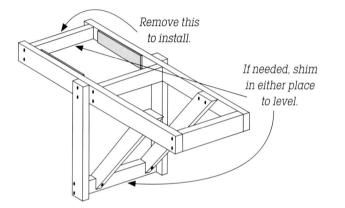

*Remove this
to install.*

*If needed, shim
in either place
to level.*

*There is considerable pull at this point.
Thus, it needs to be strong.*

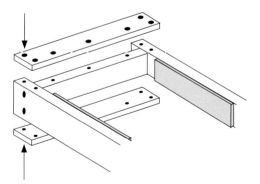

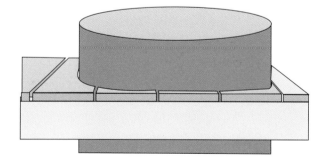

After you replace the backboard, cut and install two 3/4-inch boards above and below the backboard.

With a jigsaw, I made a loose collar around the tree with 3/4-inch boards to make a level surface all around the tree.

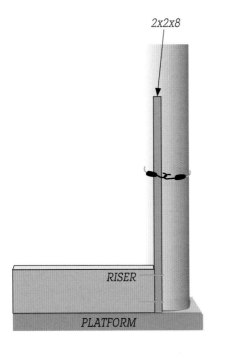

2x2x8

RISER

PLATFORM

My next task was to cut twelve pieces of 2x8 lumber for the risers. Each piece is twenty-four inches long. I used a radial saw to get a square cut.

Now the fun part begins.

Using two 4-inch deck screws (shown in red), I attached a riser to a 2x2x8—both parts resting on the platform. Strap a bungee cord around the 2x2 and trunk about five feet up to hold steady while working.

Now is the time to make some careful measurements to avoid problems later on.

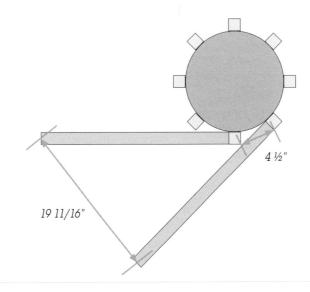

4 ½"

19 11/16"

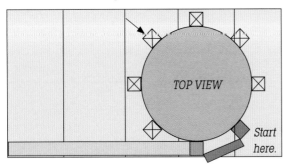

Pencil on platform floor

TOP VIEW

Start here.

Based on measurements calculated on my computer, I determined that the distance separating the outer ends of the risers should be 19 11/16 inches from center to center. The distance between the 2x2s should be 4½ inches front edge to front edge.

I cut a 2-foot length of narrow hardwood molding and drilled small holes 19 11/16 inches apart. I inserted a small wood screw in each hole and set it aside. I then cut a 4½-inch length of the same molding and a 2-foot length of 2x2.

Starting with the 4½-inch piece, lay it down as shown in the picture, place the 2-inch piece of 2x2 as shown, and trace around the 2x2. Repeat this all around the tree counterclockwise. If it comes out equal, I'm finished. If not, I'll take the last measurement that brought me full circle and determine the amount over or under. Divide it by eight and add or subtract that number from 4¼ and cut a new length of molding. Using a felt tip, measure and mark around the trunk again. This will help keep the 2x2s spaced, so that when the steps come full circle, the ends of the lower risers will be directly below the riser eight steps above. These serve to further tie the steps together and enclose the whole structure.

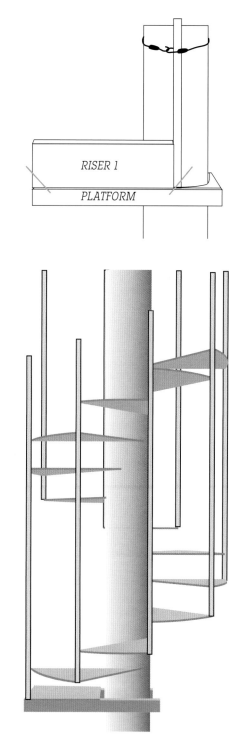

With riser 1 in position, I added two deck screws as shown below in red. This step secures the first riser. Next I made a long measuring stick from an 8-foot length of quarter round moulding to position the rest of the risers on the 2x2 uprights. Place the measuring stick upright against riser one on the platform next to the 2x2. Mark the riser top, add the thickness of the step floor boards (in my case 3/4 inch), and mark the measuring stick.

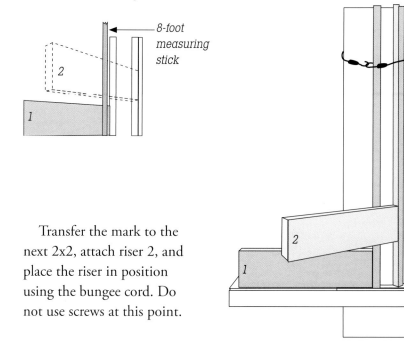

Transfer the mark to the next 2x2, attach riser 2, and place the riser in position using the bungee cord. Do not use screws at this point.

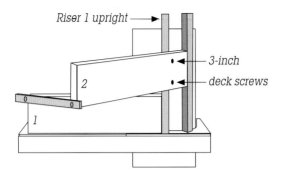

Riser 1 upright →

3-inch
deck screws

2

1

Riser 2 is now at the correct height in relation to riser 1. The next step is to position the 2x2 upright on its mark. A small screw angled in will hold it. Then make sure the bungee cord is holding it vertical. Next use the piece of hardwood with the two screws spaced 19 11/16 inches apart. Screw it to the center top of riser 1 and the center bottom of riser 2 (screw placement shown below in color).

Make sure the top of riser 2 is level by adjusting the 2x2 upright; then attach riser 2 to the 2x2 upright of riser 1 using two 3-inch deck screws.

Now is the time to install the first set of floor boards. Starting from the outside, lay a plank in position, mark with a pencil, and cut. Use 2-inch deck screws and install as shown.

Lastly, install a 2x2 as shown using 4-inch deck screws. This is necessary because of the way that the floorboards are attached to riser 2.

Riser 2 is finished. Use the same process to install the remaining risers.

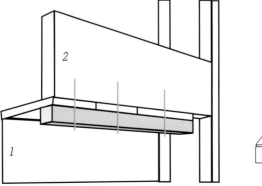

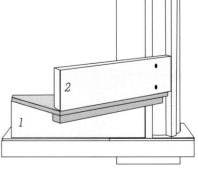

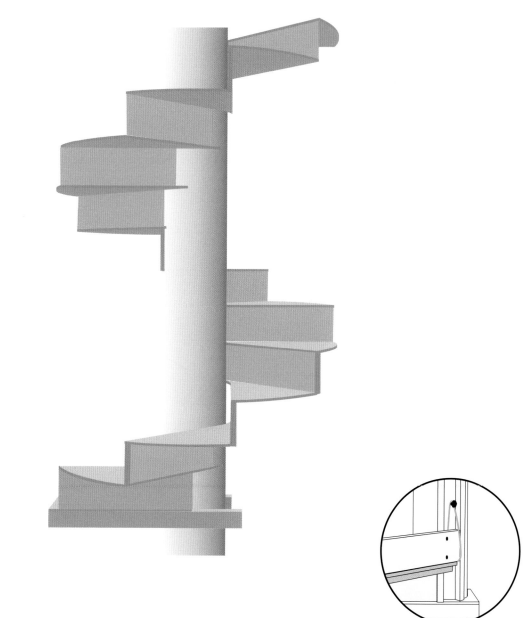

Install a support cable on every other riser. Use a
limb stub or lag screw.

Add the outer 2x2 uprights, handrails, lattice screen, and safety rope, and put a lantern at the top.

Hook up the bridge to the bottom, and then we can talk about what to do at the top. Since this can be seen from the street, I began to get visitors.

So . . . what to do at the top?

In my situation I wanted a platform suspended between the top of the staircase and a nearby tree, as shown below. Note that the new tree happened to be in line with the bridge. Other angles can be managed by adjusting the angle of the staircase anchor and or changing the number of steps. By adding four more steps I could hang a bridge going directly back over the lower bridge.

To finish the top step and support an anchor board, I installed one more 2x8 riser as shown below in color. The anchor board is also shown in the next three illustrations.

Cut the 2x8 anchor board six inches longer than the ends of the top risers. I had to trim back the last board, as shown below, so that the anchor board would be perpendicular to a line to the target tree.

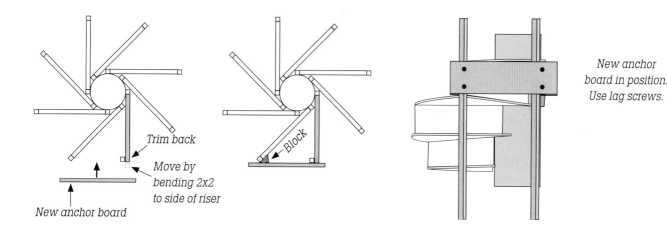

New anchor board

Trim back

Move by bending 2x2 to side of riser

Block

New anchor board in position. Use lag screws.

The new anchor is solidly in place, but it is about twenty-four feet up at a point where the trunk moves more than a couple of inches in a strong wind. I had to allow for movement as shown below.

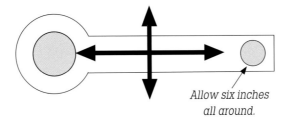

Platform moves with staircase, which moves with trunk

Allow six inches all around.

This should do it, but what if a very high wind hits from the side? This is the direction of prevailing winds in my back yard. With that in mind, I added one more flexible feature.

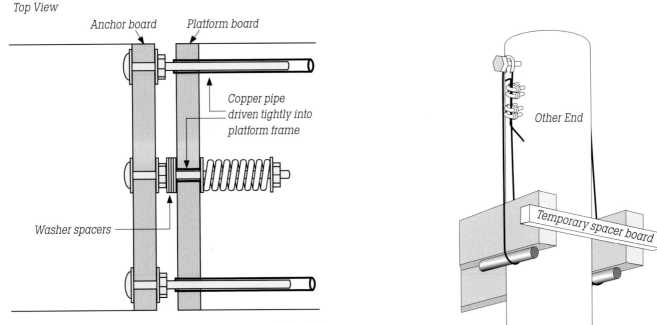

Top View

Anchor board   *Platform board*

Copper pipe driven tightly into platform frame

Washer spacers

Carriage bolts fixed to anchor board. Outside bolts slide freely in copper pipe. Center bolt spring pushes platform to stairs.

Other End

Temporary spacer board

As you can see in the diagram below, this mechanism allows the platform to bend in a high wind. The outer bolts provide support in every direction other than in and out.

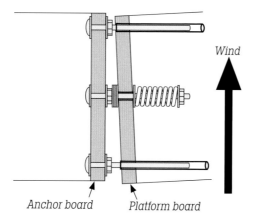

Anchor board   Platform board   Wind

This may seem excessive to some, but stick with me just a while longer. These instructions will help you build fun and safe tree houses. This section is almost finished. All that remains is to talk about the cables.

The platform starts as a rectangle tied to the staircase and hung by cables at the other end.

First, using ¼" x 4" lag screws and pilot holes, I added 2x4s to the dimension of the new tree house. In this case, it measured about four feet wide by six feet long.

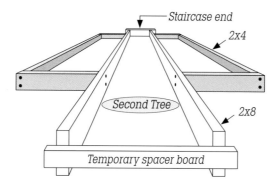

Staircase end
2x4
Second Tree
2x8
Temporary spacer board

Notice that the 2x4s do not run through the middle. This is because of the 1-inch thick decking lumber that covers the floor. Running perpendicular to the main beams, the decking makes a strong unit.

In addition to the existing cables (shown in black), add two new cables (shown in red) and anchor them to the center of the tree facing the platform.

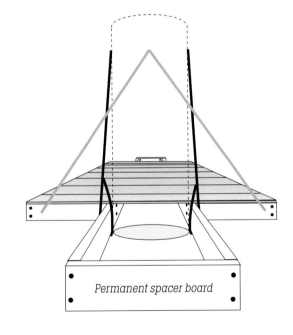

Permanent spacer board

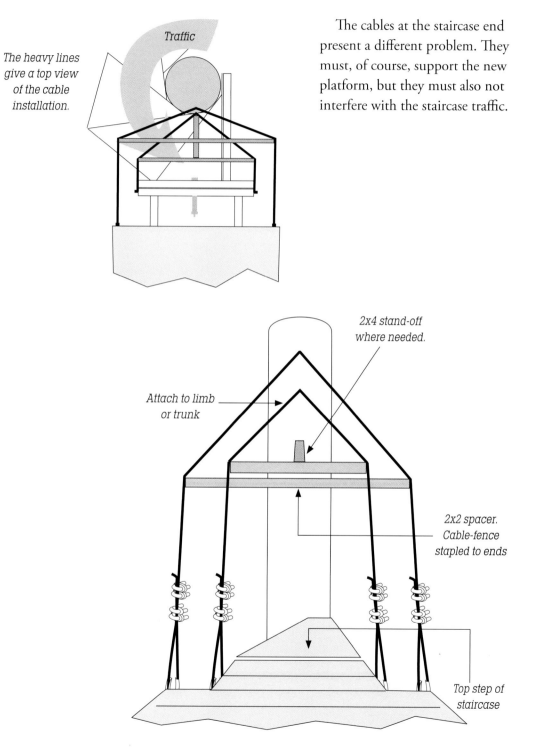

Traffic

The heavy lines give a top view of the cable installation.

The cables at the staircase end present a different problem. They must, of course, support the new platform, but they must also not interfere with the staircase traffic.

2x4 stand-off where needed.

Attach to limb or trunk

2x2 spacer. Cable-fence stapled to ends

Top step of staircase

The staircase is finished. On this illustration, I left off most of the handrails and lattice screens, as they obscure the view. I also extended some of the 2x2 uprights in order to accommodate the handrails and safety rope.

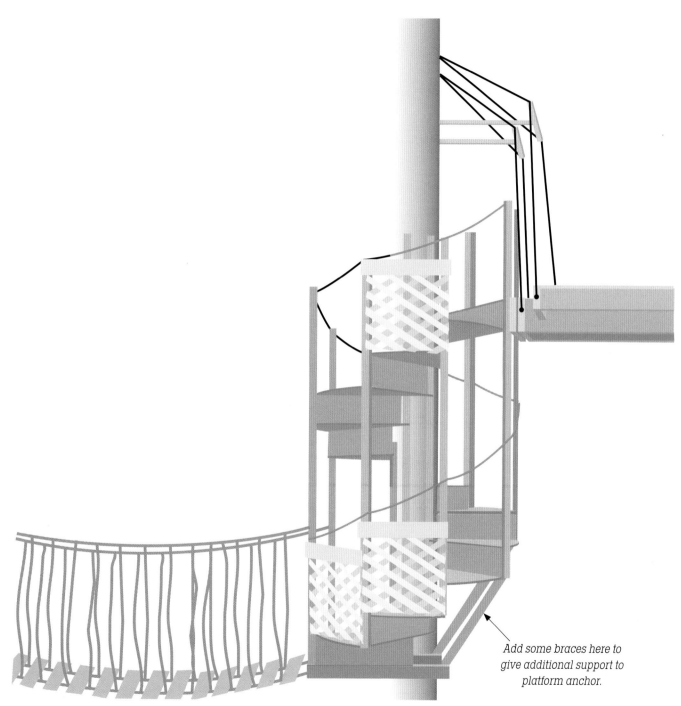

Add some braces here to give additional support to platform anchor.

Airborne Decks

On a bright, breezy summer day, this is my favorite place to sit with my coffee and just look and listen. The leaves form a cool, glowing canopy as bright splashes of sunshine and shadow dance all around. A bird may land on a nearby branch, suddenly notice my presence, squawk, and streak away. If I am alone, the only other visitor I can expect is Throckmorton, our resident squirrel. Of course I am more and more not alone. Little elves constantly scamper by on their way to the places where children go. The elves were always a part of the master plan, but the deck was not. It began in the third year and was a part of the solution to a problem that I faced.

During the first two years, I had built two tree houses and five bridges. In the fall of the second year, my last bridge of the summer carried me to the edge of my back yard. Until then the trees were reasonably close (ten to fourteen feet), which is a good distance for a rope bridge. If I wanted to continue, my only choice was a locust tree in my side yard about twenty-five feet away. (See the picture I took the following winter).

So what did I do? I did what I do best—daydream. I had a several months to plan, so I took a few pictures and settled in for the winter.

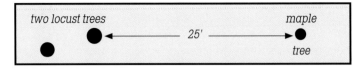

Gradually the idea of a combination rope and solid bridge took shape. I also realized that having the locust trees close together would provide support for an open, floating deck. I built it several times in my head, and when spring came I was ready.

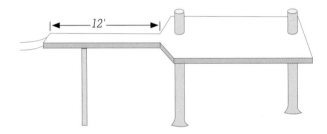

This was my basic plan. The bridge would be supported by a 4x4 post about four feet from the bridge end. The deck would be supported by the two locust trees, with lateral stability provided by two heavy branches that happen to be in the right location.

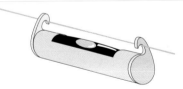

Everyone should have a string level, even if you have no immediate use for it.
It's smaller than a pencil, and it's just cool to have one.

Here's how it worked: I tied a string from the bridge base on the maple tree and ran it to a point on the closest locust trunk that brought the string to level. The solid bridge had to point directly at the maple tree. Because of its pull, the rope bridge coming from that tree will hold the entire structure in position. I wrapped masking tape around the trunk of the locust tree to preserve the mark. Using a plumb line (see illustration on the following page), I determined the location of the 4x4 bridge post and dug a hole about three feet wide by one foot deep. I dropped in some stones and some scrap iron pieces then filled it to two inches below ground level with concrete mix. When set, I mixed a little mortar and placed a square brick at the spot where the bridge post would stand. I was careful to set the brick above ground level and to level the top both ways. The next day I covered the hole with sod, leaving only the brick showing.

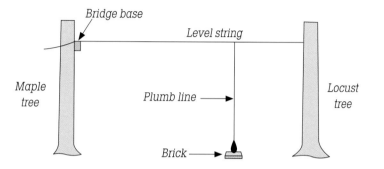

My next job was to make two 18-foot beams for the solid bridge. This required two 2x6x10 and four 2x6x8 boards. The nearest level spot was my driveway, so that's where I did the initial assembly. I butted a 10-foot to an 8-foot and then clamped another 8-foot midway over the joint. My drill and carriage bolts finished this step.

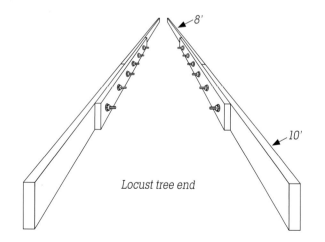

After moving the beams to the yard between the trees, I added a few 16-inch floorboards to hold the beams square while hoisting and one 2x6 that will butt up against the locust tree for positioning. Make three of these—two will be used when the bridge is up. A 2x6 bridge anchor board is bolted to the other end. Then the bridge is ready to go up.

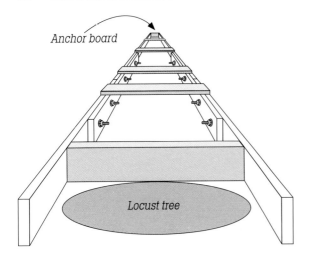

Anchor board

Locust tree

However, there are a few things to do before the big lift. Place your 4x4 post on the brick, and with the help of a friend and a stepladder, mark where the level string touches the post. The string is at the top of the walking surface of the bridge. Lay the post down; subtract the height of a 2x6 and the thickness of the floorboards and mark. This mark is the top of the cross piece that will support the bridge.

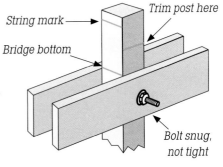

String mark

Trim post here

Bridge bottom

Bolt snug, not tight

Cut two 2x6s in 24-inch lengths and mark the center. Clamp onto post as shown above. Drill through all and install at least a 1/2-inch carriage bolt, not too tight. Place on ground as shown below then go find a couple of neighbors or other people to help lift things.

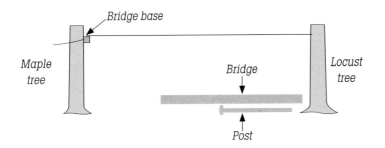

Bridge base

Maple tree

Bridge

Locust tree

Post

Luckily I have a four-pulley block and tackle as well as two young, strong neighbors. We set up the block and tackle as shown and hoisted the locust end of the bridge.

When lifted just above the mark on the locust trunk, tie off the hoist rope.

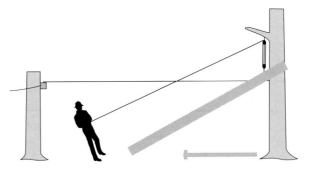

Now tie a guide rope to the lower end of the bridge and loop it over the bridge base on the maple tree. Also tie the short crosspiece, which the block and tackle is holding up, to the locust trunk to keep the bridge from pulling away from the trunk when being lifted.

Tie around trunk

Have one helper grab the guide rope and the other lift the bridge by lifting on it with the post.

When the post is vertical, tie off each side of the end with two new ropes as you would a tent; this way the bridge end won't move. Also tie off the guide rope.

Now lower the block and tackle to the mark on the trunk, which brings the bridge to level. Add two 1/4-inch cables to the bridge ends and secure to the locust trunk with 1/2" x 4" lag bolts. Remove the block and tackle.

Every spring I plant morning glories in the red planter. The vine climbs the post, the bridge sides, the ribbon staffs, and proceeds on into the tree. One year I had a friend named Jack plant pole beans.

After a nice break, go up in the locust and add two 2x6 boards, as shown below. This part must be strong, because as the rope bridge pulls the entire structure, it is at this point that the locust will provide the resistance.

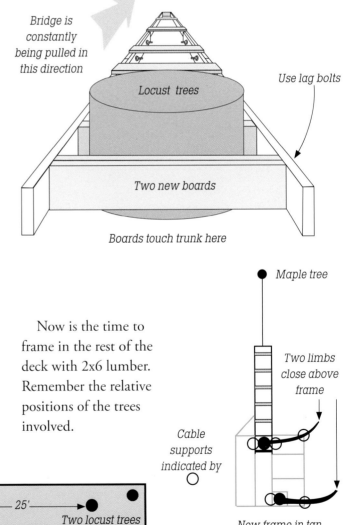

Bridge is constantly being pulled in this direction

Use lag bolts

Locust trees

Two new boards

Boards touch trunk here

Now is the time to frame in the rest of the deck with 2x6 lumber. Remember the relative positions of the trees involved.

Maple tree

Two limbs close above frame

Cable supports indicated by ○

New frame in tan

Maple tree ●◄— 25' —►● Two locust trees

This is the basic frame with the cables shown in red. Note that the cables on the right side hold the platform both up and down, in case an extra-heavy load is placed on the left.

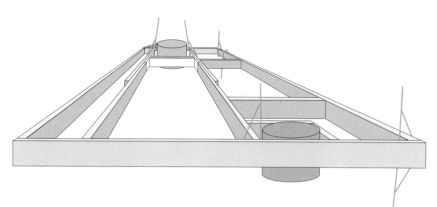

And here is the deck floor.

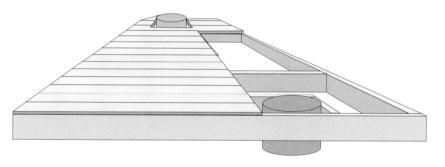

A five-sided platform and handrails finish the basic deck.

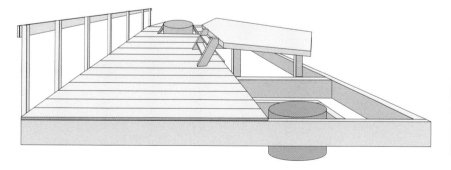

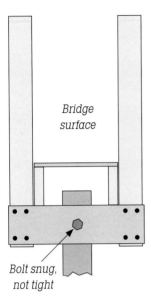

Bridge surface

Bolt snug, not tight

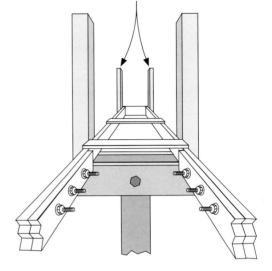

2x4 posts at end of bridge to hold hand ropes.

Now it's time to finish the combination solid and rope bridges. Make sure the post is vertical and centered. Cut an 8-foot 4x4 post in half. Attach to post crosspiece with deck screws on both sides.

For the sides, use 32-inch 2x2s. You can get three from an 8-foot length. Attach these to the outer sides of the bridge beams about one foot apart as shown. I used 3-inch deck screws, because if the point came through the bridge beam on the inside, it didn't matter. I try to use the longest possible screw.

Add a top rail of 3/4x4 lumber, lath screen, and some flags and ribbons.

Now is a good time to build the rope and plank bridge to the maple tree. Actual construction is covered in the section on bridges. The difference is the way that the hand ropes attach to the solid bridge.

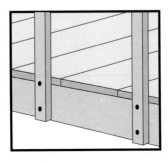

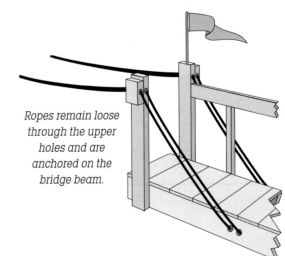

Ropes remain loose through the upper holes and are anchored on the bridge beam.

This illustration shows the levels and walking surfaces of the finished deck. These details cannot be seen in the photographs because of all those pesky leaves.

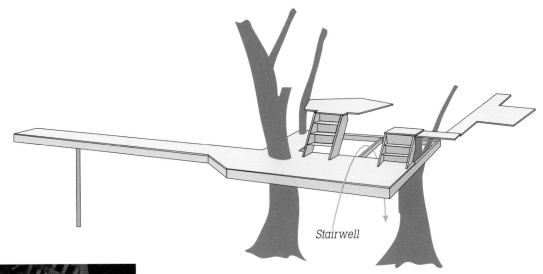

Stairwell

The odd-looking extension shown above on the far left is a walkway to Victoria's Tearoom. It has a small bench seat and countertop like half of a booth—excellent for a private meeting. At the walkway's end is a mysterious object, one of many that can be discovered here and there in the trees.

The five-sided platform shown in the illustration on the previous page was to have been the observatory. I thought it would be a good place to set up my telescope and track the moon on summer nights. I soon discovered that even in calm weather, the platform is in constant motion, however slight that motion might be. Thus, the telescope came down from the tree and a

The stairwell was an inspired idea. It eliminates the need for a long ladder and adds interest to the structure. The picture is clear enough so that a drawing is not necessary.

small table took its place. We still call it the observatory, but it is really just a nice place to sit and have a chat with a friend.

What the heck is this? ⟶

Well . . . I had to make some seats to enclose the observatory. My thought was to make something open, tent-like, and whimsical. I can't explain how I created this design, but I like it.

My first project was a platform surrounding a tree with three trunks. At that point in time I had no real ideas; I just wanted to get something up for the grandkids. It is just a straightforward construction using a 2x6 frame and the smaller landscape timbers for the corner posts.

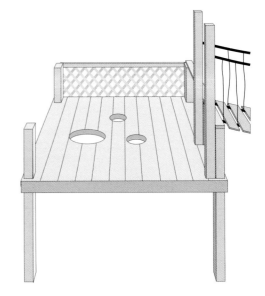

Houses

This section deals with the support mechanism for lollipop houses. The houses are covered in the house design and building section.

When I finished the floating deck, I would have liked a tree house in that area, but I had no more trees and I could not go up. So after

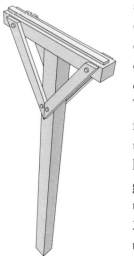

another serious bout of daydreaming, I came up with the idea of a house on a stick, or a lollipop house. The structure is made from 6x6 landscape timbers and 2x4 treated lumber. I used 1/2"x5" galvanized lag screws on the diagonal supports. A 2x4 is deck screwed to the top.

Here are the details:

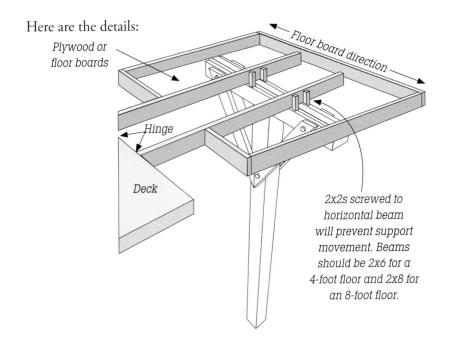

Plywood or floor boards

Hinge

Deck

2x2s screwed to horizontal beam will prevent support movement. Beams should be 2x6 for a 4-foot floor and 2x8 for an 8-foot floor.

All lateral support is provided by the deck. As the deck moves in any direction, the house goes along for the ride.

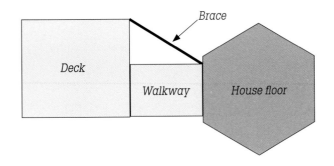

Brace

Deck

Walkway

House floor

The post under the house provides total support for the weight.

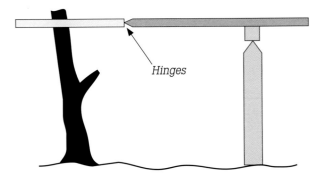

Hinges

The exaggerated view below shows how the system of hinges works.

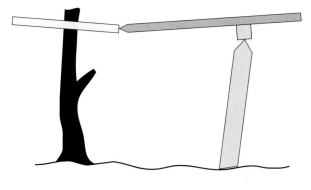

In actual use, the hinges hardly move at all. I have one system that has been in use for three years and has proved very effective.

Heavy duty strap hinge

Building Houses
The houses in this section appear in the order in which they were built.

I build little houses for little people. Tiny structures please everyone, even adults who have to scrunch and twist a bit to enter. The miniature size enhances the magic of curious little places tucked here and there in the trees. My houses are not tall. They are built in the winter in my basement where the ceiling is seven feet from the floor. Once built they must easily come apart for the trip up the cellar stairs, but I have a system that works and fits well with the buildings that I create. All houses have doors that close, windows with screens, plenty of miniature seating, low voltage electric lights, and many mysterious objects. I try to include things that can be used safely by little fingers.

Mary's Teahouse

This was my first attempt at a real tree house. I have the written testimony of a great number of "experts in the field" who grade the house a ten out of ten. Of course they are all under the age of ten, but those are my customers. In this part of the book I will describe my thought processes as well as my actions during construction.

First, the shape.

I like round buildings and towers, but they are more difficult to fabricate so I chose to build a tree house with six sides and within the confines of my basement. The original diameter was about five feet. I decided to add one foot to the length so that a 6-foot person could lie down and stretch out.

Final floor plan.

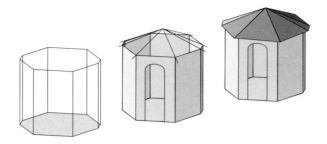

As for the walls, I decided to make them five feet high. The roof shown fit quite well in to the teahouse theme, and I had my basic shape.

The inside had to have smooth walls for a finished look. The outside was a problem. I did not want plain external walls. My solution was to use ¾x4s instead of 2x4s and to forgo applying any covering to the walls.

My life as a packrat served me well when I went looking for something to use for windows. A few years before, we had remodeled our kitchen. I removed the grillwork over the cabinets and tucked it away in the basement. Luckily, the grill widths were a very close fit—just a little trimming was needed. I boxed in a window frame, put aluminum screening over the grill backs, and then fixed the grill on the outside. That done, I applied four sculptured, plastic panels below the grills. These I had salvaged from some old furniture.

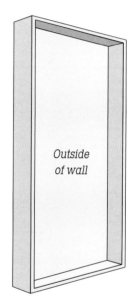

Outside of wall

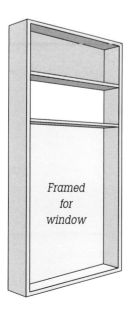

Framed for window

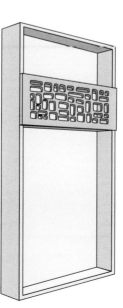

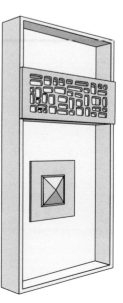

The two small center panels were treated the same. An old black plastic tube was cut to fit under the grill. The illustration below is a side view.

My last wall inspiration is shown below. I added shingles above the grill.

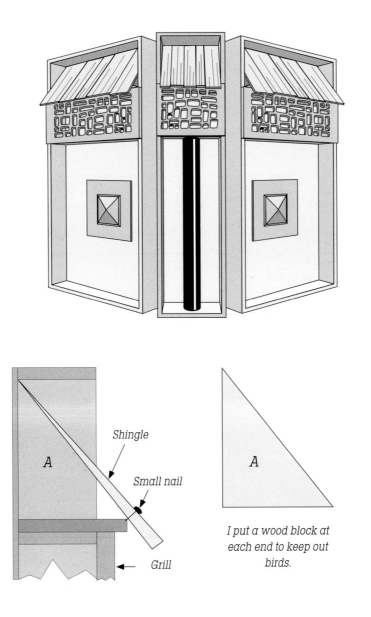

Shingle

A

Small nail

A

I put a wood block at each end to keep out birds.

Grill

The first panel below is an inside view. Note that the sunken grill provides for a nice shelf to hold all sorts of tree house stuff. The small black object above the grill is a low voltage electric light. More about that in the section on lighting.

This middle illustration shows what I did for the front.

The last illustration shows the inside back wall and the alcove I built there. It has a chandelier and other mysterious objects.

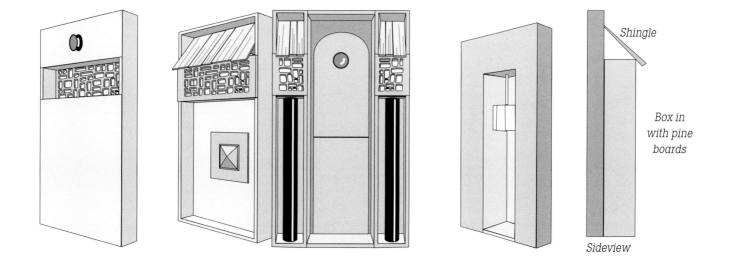

Shingle

Box in with pine boards

Sideview

In these progress shots you can see my confined workspace. The basement ceiling clearance is seven feet. Things are crowded and cluttered, but I have light, heat, and a good radio.

Since I had to disassemble the house to haul it up the tree, I developed my own little construction system that has worked quite well. The base was built first with 2x4s and 1/2-inch plywood. I did not use treated wood, because the end result was either painted or out of the weather. Also, it is not a part of any support structure.

Decide where the front door will be, get a marker, and mark the front on the wood. It will be painted over later.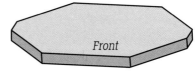

Build and install a panel. Mark it #1. Use two screws on the bottom. More will be used for reassembly in the tree. Continue counterclockwise and install the remaining panels.

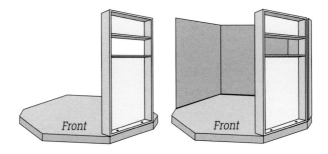

Looking down at the top of the panels, cut 1/4-inch plywood as shown and screw it in to hold the panels together.

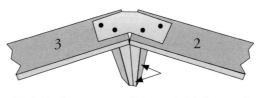

Up in the tree, screws will be angled in here and the seam caulked.

The roof was difficult for me, because I am not a cabinetmaker. I don't like to fuss until final decoration. My method works, but I'm sure many readers could do much better.

The eight rafters are 2x3 pine and the eight roof panels are 1/4-inch luan (type of wood) or whatever I have laying around.

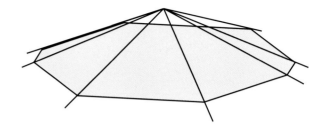

Find and mark center of floor. Drop a plum bob or a nut on a string. Place two lengths of scrap lumber about two inches apart as shown and mark string position on boards. Screw boards in place temporarily.

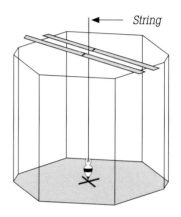

Cut a 12-inch disk from 1/2-inch plywood. Draw a 6-inch circle in the middle.

Now is the time to use one's eyeball.

Hold the disk and a rafter as shown. Raise and lower the disk until you see a slope (pitch) that you like. Have your chief assistant measure the distance from the floor to the bottom of the disk.

Cut a length of 2x2 lumber to match this measurement and screw the center of the disk to one end. Place as shown. Loosen screws at one end of scrap boards and squeeze them together so that they contact the upright. Screw down the ends of the scrap boards, then anchor the upright to the scrap boards using clamps, screws, or whatever you have on hand.

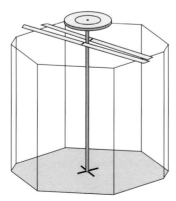

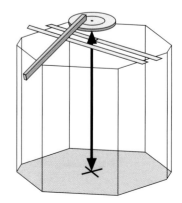

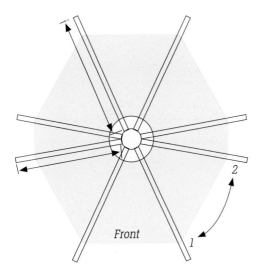

Front

2

1

Note: When the roof is finished in the tree, I removed the center pole before the last roof panel was installed. I then installed a larger 1/4-inch plywood disk below the 12-inch disk. I cut out the middle and put in a light fixture that works with the skylights.

This top view shows the rafter positions. Measure from the edge of the 6-inch circle to a point six inches beyond the outer wall. The overhang is, of course, arbitrary. Four long rafters will have the same measurement, as will the four shorter rafters. Stopping the rafters at the edge of the 6-inch circle eliminates the need to shape those ends.

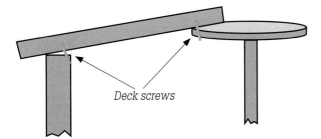

Deck screws

Start at the right edge of panel 1 and work around counterclockwise, numbering each rafter as you go.

1

Starting as shown, cut plywood roof panels to fit. Overlap rafters halfway. Seams need not be tight, as the surface can be covered with roofing tar or shingles if you wish. Work counterclockwise and number each panel.

The above space is open, which is good for ventilation. When the house is reassembled in the tree, put aluminum screening in this area.

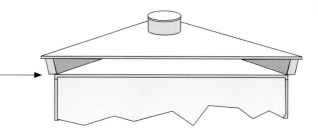

I put a skylight in each of the larger roof panels.

I used large coffee cans with the milky white plastic tops. With tin snips, cut them down to about six inches. Cut slots about 1-inch deep and wide, and peal back every other tab as shown.

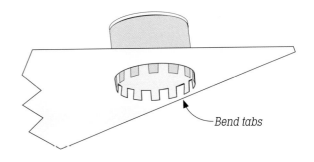

Cut a hole in the roof panel, spread plastic roof cement around the top of the hole, insert can, and bend the tabs to secure.

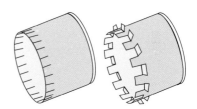

Bend tabs

Save a stack of the plastic lids. They only last for a couple of years, but they do an excellent job of illuminating the interior.

I found a green glass bowl in my vast supply of stuff. It made a perfect cap for my roof. After final assembly in the tree, I spread some roof cement at the center and placed it there upside down.

I cut a door shape from the front panel and used it as a pattern to make a Dutch door from 3/4-inch plywood.

Pattern

Door opens out

Inside view

Hinges are fixed to this board.

This board 3/8 inch to stop door.

This board flush with panel cut.

My favorite way to secure a door.

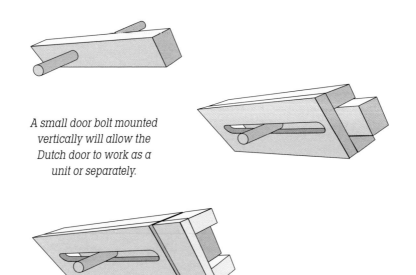

A small door bolt mounted vertically will allow the Dutch door to work as a unit or separately.

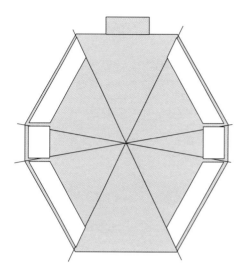

I built six small seats for the interior. The illustration shows the relative size and location.

Here is my basic design for seats. There are four pieces of wood. Use waterproof glue and screws. It helps to have a good radial or chop saw for square cuts.

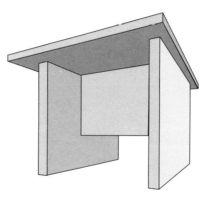

When I finished construction, I took the house apart in reverse order. (Every piece has a number.) In the tree, I assembled it in the same order in which it had been built. I painted the floor with bright red enamel and the roof with unfibered roof coating. The seams between panels got a coat of plastic roof cement. I also put the roof coating on the sides of the coffee cans. I installed the lights, added a few more touches, and opened for business.

Church in the Pines

This project is a combination of impressions that have lodged in my head over the years. All I took with me to my basement workshop was the dimensions of the platform waiting at the top of the spiral staircase. Eventually I penciled in a plan that pleased my wife, so I went to work.

A sturdy platform was up and finished, so I did not need to build a base. With a marker, I drew a rectangle to size on the cement floor in my workshop. I used 2x3 lumber for frame support. These were glued and nailed to the back wall panel

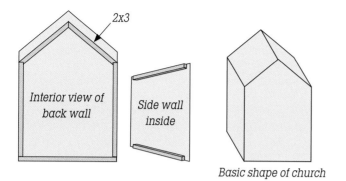

2x3

Interior view of back wall

Side wall inside

Basic shape of church

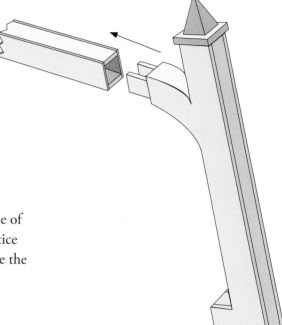

The above picture shows the four sides in place along with some of the six flying buttresses (these buttresses are purely cosmetic). Notice that I have started to make a double wall in front. I wanted to give the front windows some depth.

These are made with plywood and 1x3 strapping lumber. On final assembly in the tree, the buttress slides into the roof buttress and is held in place with screws. The bottom just rests against the side of the church.

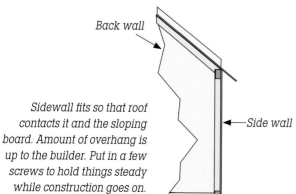

Back wall

Sidewall fits so that roof contacts it and the sloping board. Amount of overhang is up to the builder. Put in a few screws to hold things steady while construction goes on.

Side wall

Cut and assemble front and back panels as shown. The roof will be fixed to these boards. The distance below the top edge of the panel is determined by the dimensions of the buttresses.

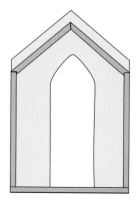

After final assembly the piece in the doorway is cut away.

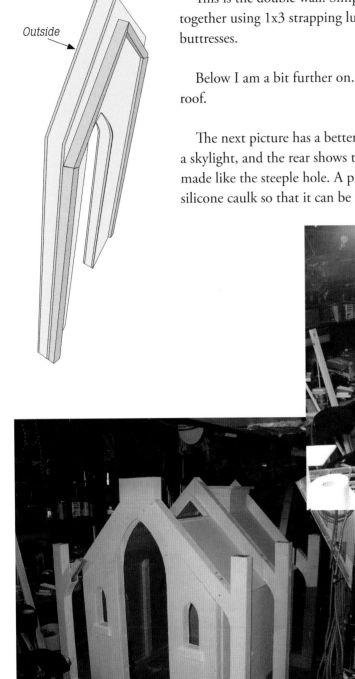

Outside

This is the double wall. Simply make two identical panels and sandwich them together using 1x3 strapping lumber in the middle. It's the same way I made the buttresses.

Below I am a bit further on. The front panel is complete, as well as much of the roof.

The next picture has a better view of the roof. The front half of the roof is cut for a skylight, and the rear shows the box structure for the steeple. The skylight hole is made like the steeple hole. A piece of bent Plexiglas is held in place with two dabs of silicone caulk so that it can be removed for maintenance.

Here's how I made the box support for the steeple. Place two scrap boards on the roof as shown. Clamp, then screw together. This provides the correct roof angle to cut box.

I made the box about a foot square. This is only a suggested measurement, as is the height.

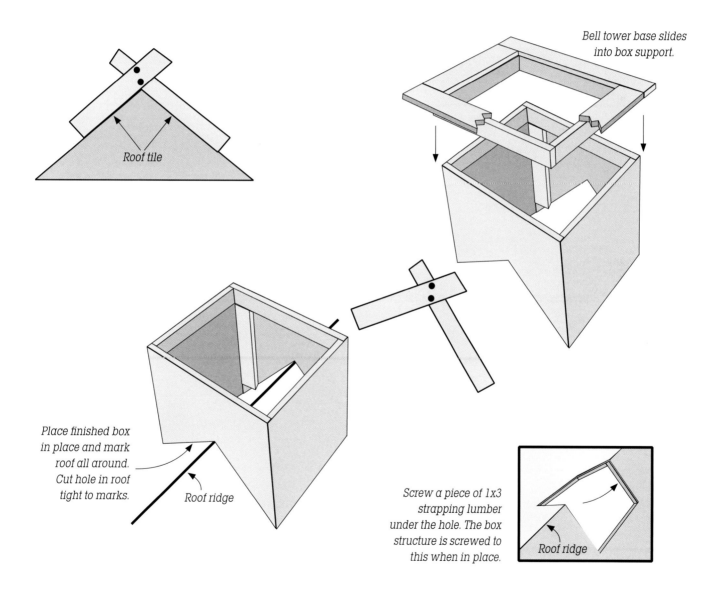

Roof tile

Bell tower base slides into box support.

Place finished box in place and mark roof all around. Cut hole in roof tight to marks.

Roof ridge

Screw a piece of 1x3 strapping lumber under the hole. The box structure is screwed to this when in place.

Roof ridge

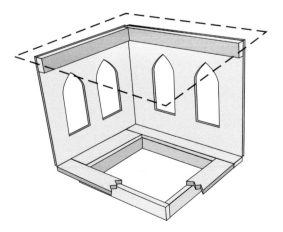

In the above picture I have added the bell tower, which is a simple rectangle built around the bell tower base. It was attached only for the picture at that stage. Later, I put the steeple on the tower and thereafter it sat on the floor until it was moved to the tree. I also added some color and window trim.

Build the bell tower and add a solid plywood top with a 1-inch overhang. The steeple sits on this plywood.

The church was all but complete when I took this picture. The door is a double door faced with plywood cutouts painted white.

The buttress tops are capped with a square of wood topped by a cardboard cone filled with plastic foam and sprayed gold.

Building the steeple was awkward, but since no one would see it up close I was able to fudge a bit here and there. I cut four plywood triangles and applied 1x1 pieces to two panels with glue and brads as shown below; then I nailed the four pieces together.

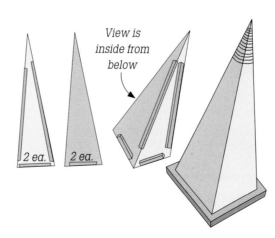

View is inside from below

2 ea.

2 ea.

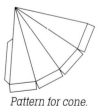

Pattern for cone.

At the peak, I pumped in some caulk then wrapped it with fine wire. The unit was then screwed to the plywood top of the bell tower.

To finish the house, I built a small feature, like a sort of pediment, at the peak above the door. I have no idea what it is officially called, but it makes a cubbyhole where I have put a small decorative image. I painted the roof with five coats of good white paint, instead of using black tar. The church has been in the tree for several seasons and all is so far-so good.

The interior is painted all white. I built an elaborate shelf to serve as an alter and put together two small benches to serve as pews.

The benches are about two feet wide, with the seat about one foot high. The depth is about eight inches, but these dimensions can be altered to fit. I cut the sides with a jig saw, drilled the holes with one of those drills used to install door knobs, and ran a router over all edges to guard against splinters. It was not fine carpentry, but they look just great.

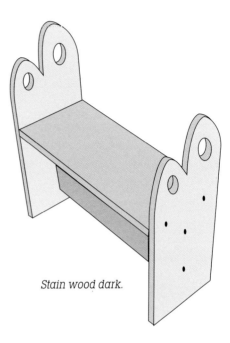

Stain wood dark.

The windows are a standard arch shape with fake stained glass windows. I used Plexiglas and made stained glass patterns with masking tape and

Krylon Stained Glass paint. The blue 1/4-inch plywood frame inside is the same as the frame outside. I had earlier glued the outside frame to the church wall. I held the window and inside frame in place and drilled a 1/8-inch hole through all four pieces and then stuck a nail through the hole to maintain position. Three more holes and nails are sufficient. Replace each nail with a small bolt with the nut on the outside. Done.

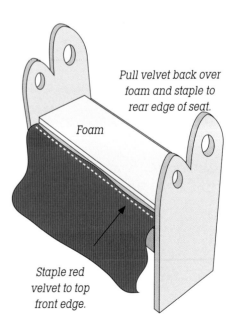

Pull velvet back over foam and staple to rear edge of seat.

Foam

Staple red velvet to top front edge.

For illumination, I used a string of ten low-voltage yard lights. Three are placed outside in lanterns, and the rest are inside the church. I put one in the bell tower, two around the altar, and one above each side window. See the section on illumination for more details.

A piece of linoleum for the floor finished the job. The existing platform has some small spaces between the boards. Bees love to enter through these spaces, so the linoleum prevents them from stinging visitors. Add some beads, jewels, gold cups, and other mystical objects and the church is ready.

Shadows

A house called Shadows. This house continues the six-sided, round shape but it is a bit different.

The base is a simple hexagon using 2x4 lumber. This shape and the five small extensions were cut from two sheets of 1/2-inch plywood. The extensions hang out but support no weight. The fine radiating lines represent the eighteen rafters of this rather complex roof. The photo below of the snow-covered roof is a good illustration of how the roof panels are angled.

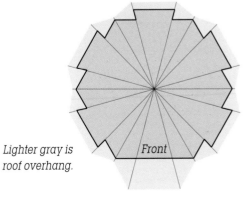

Lighter gray is roof overhang.

Front

The illustration below shows how 2x2 lumber is cut in half the long way at the appropriate angle to join the sides. I used waterproof glue and brads to join them.

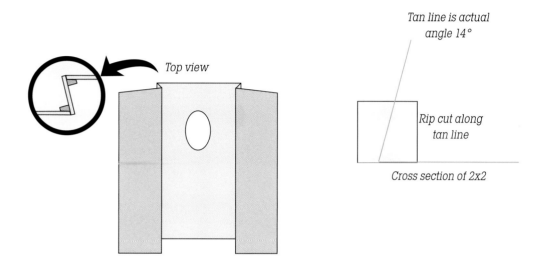

Top view

Tan line is actual angle 14°

Rip cut along tan line

Cross section of 2x2

Here is the pattern for the 2x3 lumber that will be at the bottom and top of the panels. The 2x3 boards on the bottom rest on top of the plywood base. Build this one panel at a time, starting with the front, and work around either way. Apply the 2x3 boards to the top and bottom of each panel before fixing it to the base.

Number each panel for reassembly.

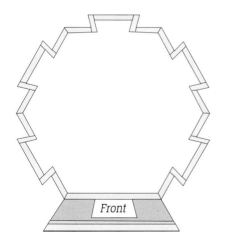

Front

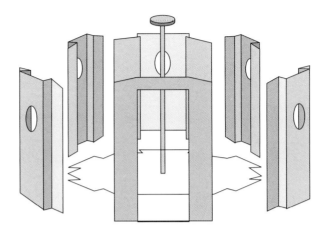

Note that some of the 2x3 boards used on the top do not lie in a flat plane but follow the contours of the top.

Note: The panel tops must be sloped to give the roof its unique shape. The angle of slope is exaggerated for clarity although the angle can be whatever the builder wishes.

The illustration to the left shows how the panels must come apart for the trip to the tree. The panels with the windows consist of five strips of plywood that are permanently glued and nailed together.

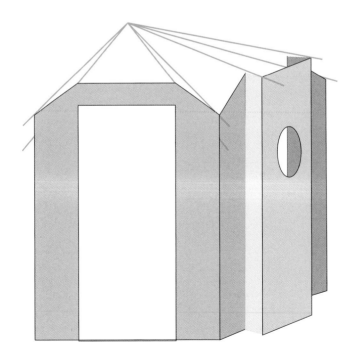

The following shows how the wood strips that join the completed panels together are cut, glued, and nailed to one side only. A couple of small screws are used on the other side during assembly.

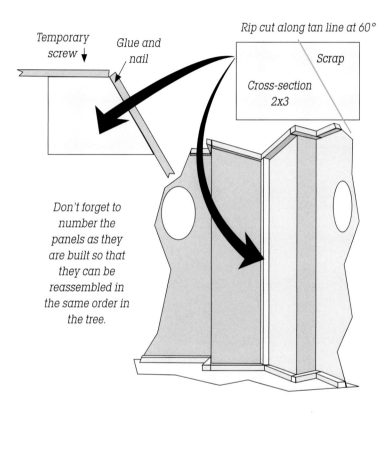

Temporary screw ↓

Glue and nail

Rip cut along tan line at 60°

Scrap

Cross-section
2x3

Don't forget to number the panels as they are built so that they can be reassembled in the same order in the tree.

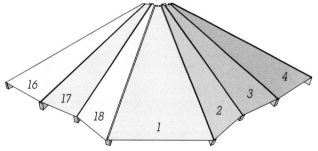

16

17

18

1

2

3

4

Now that the walls are up, it's time to install the rafters. Start from the front and work around, numbering them as they are put in place. It's a good idea to also put the number on the center disk and where they rest on the outside wall. The front two rafters overhang the walls by about twenty inches, while the rest overhang ten inches.

The next step is to measure and cut the eighteen plywood roof panels. Since I am fussy only where necessary, most of the panels don't butt smoothly. They will be covered with roof cement so no one will see the wiggly seam. The roof panels should run out to the ends of the rafters and up to the center disk. The center will be covered with aluminum screening and a fancy vent placed on top. Number the panels on the top surface.

Cut the large suspended shadow panels and paint them. (They can be seen in the photographs, but they are blue on the blue house.) Don't mount them until the house is in the tree. The panels are placed using wires to the rafter ends and the base. Red lines below indicate wires. Make sure to use strong wires.

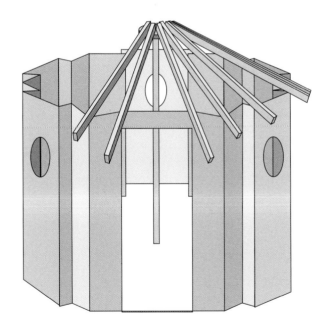

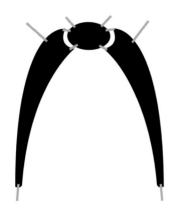

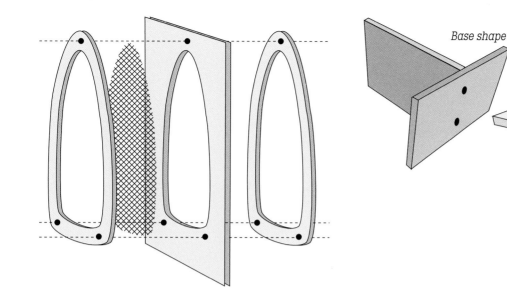

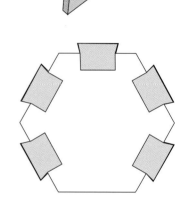

Base shape

Finished seat

Decide on a shape for the windows, draw it to size on card stock, and cut it out for a template. Trace it in position on the panel, then jigsaw the hole. Make a 1-inch frame from the same plywood. Make two frame shapes for each window: one for the outside and one for the inside. Cut a piece of aluminum screening larger than the window opening.

Clamp the frames in position without the screening, and drill three holes for bolts. Remove clamps, apply adhesive caulk to both frames, lay the screen in place, (get a helper to hold the inside frame in place), position the outside frame, insert the bolts from the inside, and tighten. I use this method for most windows. If anyone has an easier solution, please give me a call.

I came up with a nifty idea for the seats in Shadows. They are cut to fit snuggly into the extensions. This serves to lock the seats in place. To remove, simply lift and tip.

The seats don't need backs as they fit only tight to the wall. A piece of rug cut to fit the top works well.

The center pole remains in this house, so I made a "table-table." The disks are screwed to small triangles of wood, which in turn are screwed to the center pole.

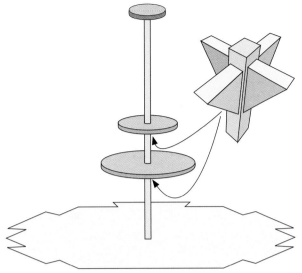

Now that I had a "table-table," wouldn't it be nice to have a "door-door"? Yes. The large door is held closed by an unobtrusive sliding peg on the upper right side. (See Mary's Teahouse for a drawing of the peg lock.) The door itself is painted the same color as the wall so that the new visitor won't notice it. The small door in the middle bottom of the large door is painted gold with fancy trim. A five year old can walk through the gold door with no room to spare. When grown-ups protest, I tell them of the hidden door. What fun! Works like a charm.

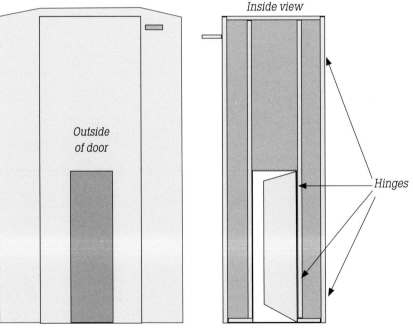

Shadows uses a string of ten 4-watt, low-voltage yard lights. Four of them are inside. Six lights mounted low on the outside walls point up to illuminate the walls. (See photo.) The last two lights were put in hanging lanterns near the door.

The lights above are bare 4-watt bulbs in the top of 6-inch black plastic tubes that I had laying around. They shine down on the "table-table" and create even more shadows. See the section on lighting for more information.

Dream up an unusual design for the top—simple or complex. Use screening for ventilation. Paint it gold, place it at the roof peak, and secure it with a couple of screws.

Chelsea's Gazebo

Close to the southwest corner of my house is a good-sized maple tree. It is also reasonably near the trees that host my tree village, so it was a logical choice for my next structure. The maple is too far for a single rope bridge, so I built a combination solid-and-rope bridge similar to the one I built for the first tree deck. The rope bridge is the same as the others, but the solid part is different because I used lumber that I had in my inventory.

A while back, a kind person had given me a single 16-foot 2x12 beam. It is a very strong, single piece of wood. Now, it is necessary that I be frugal. Good wood is quite expensive, so I try to be creative and this is one example. The same kind person had also given me three 16-foot 1x6 lengths of treated pine.

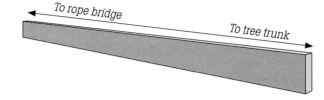

I used the big beam and two of the smaller pieces as shown here in cross section. The sidepieces are fixed to the floor planks, which in turn are fixed to the large beam.

As shown in the next illustration, I decided to hang the trunk end of the beam like a hammock. Note that the center post has a spade-like board bolted to its top to keep the bridge floor from tipping side to side. Refer to the section on decks for information on lifting and leveling the superstructure.

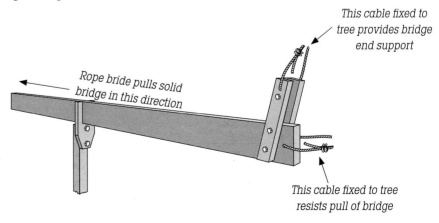

Next, bolt a 2x8 anchor board to the rope bridge end. Pre-drill the rope holes. Screw one floorboard to the tree end and then install the two side beams.

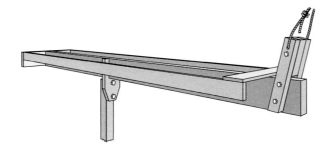

Install the remaining floorboards, handrails, and rope hand supports. That done, build the rope bridge as described in the bridge chapter.

The maple tree involved here is half the size of what it would be if it were not so close to my house. Over time, I have trimmed the branches that tried to grow over the roof. The result is a curious arrangement of branches that all tend to grow to the east. I thought that it might be a good idea to have more than one thing at this new destination. The overhead view is phase one, which I finished in one summer.

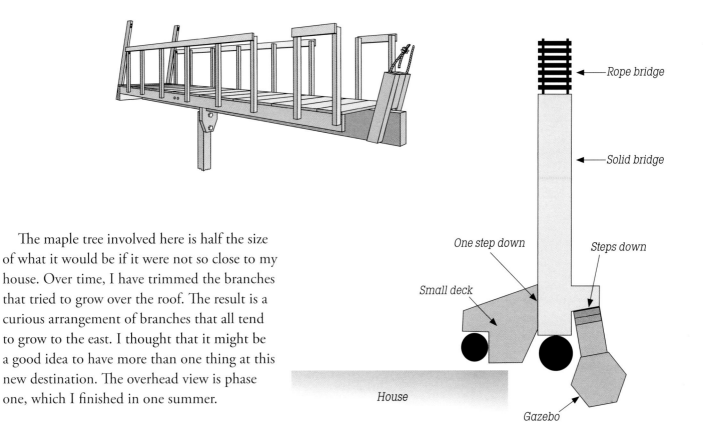

A few years later, I built a larger tree house (The Wizard's Den) above the small deck and a walkway to the second floor of our real, full-size house. Permanently connecting the walkway to the house would require the removal of a second-story window and the installation of a door. I could do that, but I didn't. I am a practical man; I know my limits and I know the zoning laws.

The gazebo and small deck are lower than the bridge floor and at an angle. I will show the construction with photographs rather than drawings, because trying to draw it could drive a person crazy.

Above, the deck 2x4s are bolted to the main bridge beam and fan out for the deck.

The photo on the previous page is a front view of steps leading down to the gazebo. Also note the aircraft cable support, which wraps under the gazebo walkway and is fixed to a large limb directly overhead. The little gazebo sits suspended at the end of the walkway.

The finished and decorated Gazebo. This photo was taken in October. Things will look ever so much better in the summer.

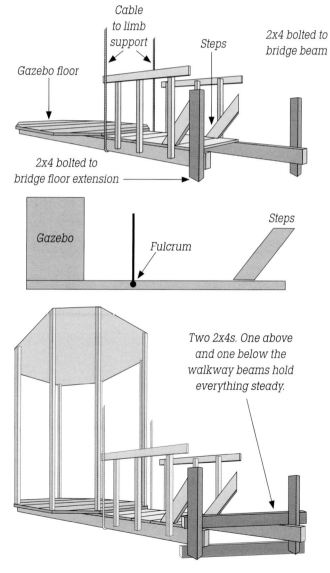

Cable to limb support

Steps

2x4 bolted to bridge beam

Gazebo floor

2x4 bolted to bridge floor extension

Gazebo

Fulcrum

Steps

Two 2x4s. One above and one below the walkway beams hold everything steady.

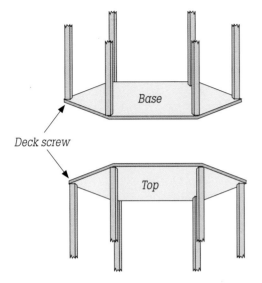

OK, I see that I'll have to draw some of the construction for clarification. Above is the basic support and walkway for the gazebo.

Once you have finished the base unit, it's time to construct the gazebo. Using the floor hexagon pattern, cut two more pieces of wood from 1/2-inch plywood for use on the bottom and top. Cut six 2x2 uprights to the height you desire. Deck screw them to the base. This done, deck screw one of the plywood hexagons to the top.

At this point, the structure is quite wobbly. Tie the top to nearby branches to hold it vertical, then apply lath and horizontal boards as shown in the finished photo. This will make the unit rigid.

Now build the roof. Cut six identical shapes (I used 1x6 lumber) of your choice and deck screw them to the last piece of hexagonal plywood.

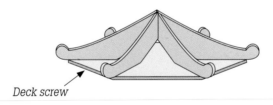

Deck screw

Cover the roof with triangular pieces; I used roofing paper to see how long it would last. You might want to use 1/8-inch plywood. Staple them in place.

Cover each roofing joint with thin wood strips. Fix a small glass bowl upside down at the peak with silicone caulk and screws or small nails. I put a light bulb in mine for added flair. Screw the unit to the top and you are ready to decorate.

I cut 1/2-inch x 1/2-inch sticks to fit as shown. Glue and a small nail hold them in place. These are purely decorative.

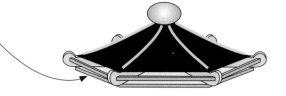

There is room inside Chelsea's Gazebo for only one chair. I added a small shelf on either side to hold books and lemonade. A beaded curtain of blue dolphins adds a nice touch.

Just who is this Chelsea person and why does she merit her own private gazebo?

Chelsea is a little girl who was a neighborhood sweetheart and a cancer survivor. A few years ago, she was diagnosed with bone cancer in one leg. The growth and some bone were removed surgically, followed by a long period of therapy, including radiation treatments. They seemed to be successful and we were all very hopeful for her future, but the cancer returned and she did not survive.

Her gazebo is there, used by many children. Chelsea has gone, but we remember.

Buddha

One day, while poking around the dollar store, I ran across an image of Buddha. That got me thinking. I have a church; why not have a Buddha tree house? So I started the process of turning the idea into a physical structure. I won't include my pencil sketches, but I will include my final computer drawings. Some dimensions were constantly subject to change. I was able to draw this to scale on my computer, so I had all of the basic measurements before I cut the first piece.

This new house was to be located on a second-floor corner of a platform. The space was thus restricted to the existing area, which was not that big; luckily, this design works well as a small room. I had a few sheets of old dark mahogany panels that were just right for the interior; I wanted the inside to be dim. The only light would come from cubbyhole altars in the walls and from a fixture in the head. Since the platform has a floor, I did not have to build a base, I drew the base dimensions on my shop floor with a square, a straight edge, and a marker. Then I went to work.

Basic elements:
After basement construction, the unit comes apart as shown for the trip to the tree.

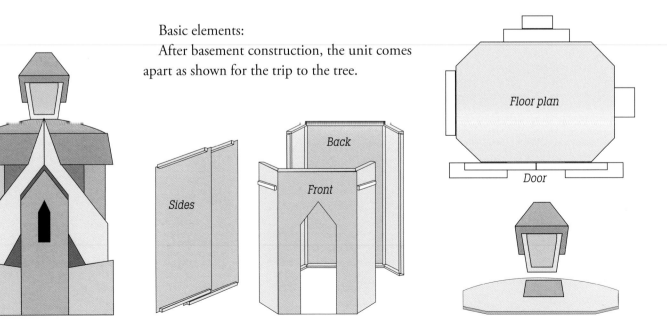

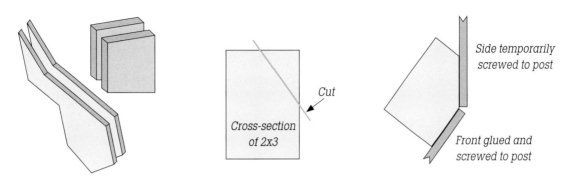

Cross-section
of 2x3

Cut

Side temporarily
screwed to post

Front glued and
screwed to post

First I built the front and back, as they are identical except for the door on the front and a cut out on the back. I framed the inside with 2x3 lumber. The vertical strips had to be rip cut at 45°.

The ornamental shapes are cut from plywood and framed with 1x3 pine boards. Cut four pieces of each to cover both sides. It keeps the bugs out. During construction, do not fix these four pieces to the front. Wait until final installation. The lower box shapes are framed with 1x4 pine boards, as they need to be thicker.

When you reach this stage, it's time to cut a shape for the door. With the ornamental objects carefully centered in position, mark the door shape on the front panel. Be sure to allow for clearance on the sides and the top. The door top clearance should be at least two inches to avoid collision with the ornamental shapes when the door is opened.

Give the exterior a coat of good, white exterior primer. You could wait until later, but for me it is an encouraging preview.

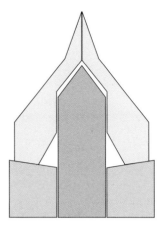

This photo shows an interior view of the side and back walls.

The photo at right is of the exterior of the right wall.

Note the hole in the wall is full width but only comes up halfway. I will cap the back and fix a piece of clear Plexiglas on the top. This will provide indirect light for the little altar. I plan on installing a small electric light for after dark. The other side and the back will have altars of different shapes.

This progress shot shows the roof frame and head support. A few inches below are the horizontal strips that make the collar blocks angle out as shown in the next photo. The collar blocks are made from small pieces of pine, rounded at the bottom corners.

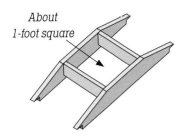

*About
1-foot square*

The top is a frame made from 1x8 pine boards. The square shape in the middle will mate to the base of the head. This will remain open so that once inside, the viewer can look up and see the interior of the head.

Assemble in position and mark frame front for proper assembly in the tree. Do not fasten to top of walls.

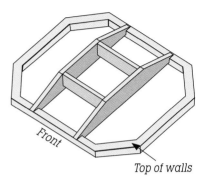

Front

Top of walls

Add four more pieces as shown. Then frame is complete.

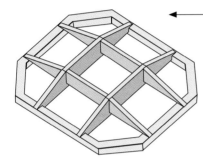

Lay a piece of scrap plywood over the center hole and trace the square opening from below. This is the pattern to form the neck of the head so that the two units will mate on final assembly.

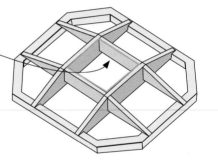

The roof sheeting is eight pieces of plywood. Make the four rectangular pieces first. Measure and cut each piece. If you build like I do, the dimensions of each area will not be the same. Each piece will butt to the outer edge of the box and the outer edges of the walls with the collars in place.

*Sides will
overlap
the frame
boards half
way. Mark
each piece
and tack in
place.*

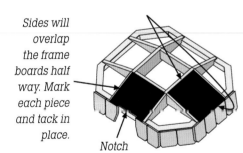

Notch

The corner pieces present another problem. Again, each one must be measured separately. Start with a piece of plywood larger than the area to be covered. It should have one straight edge. Lay the good edge on the left as shown. Plywood should lay flat along the dashed red line. Draw this line from underneath and mark corner indicated by circle.

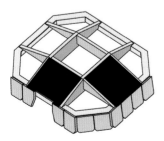

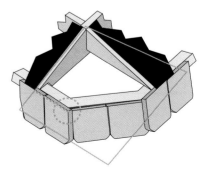

Hold the top and rock the plywood so that it rests flat on the middle section indicated by the dashed red line. Draw line and mark next corner.

Rotate again and mark as before. The last corner mark will be one end of the cut line where the new piece butts to the roof piece on the right.

Now connect the marks and cut.

Draw two lines as shown on the top of the plywood and score cut. That is, set your radial saw to cut half way through the plywood. This allows you to bend the piece to conform to the shape of the roof. Mark and tack in place. Take a picture for your records. Who knows—someday you may write a book.

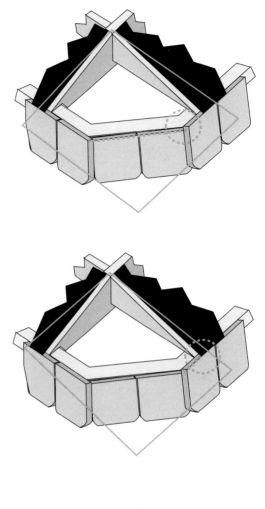

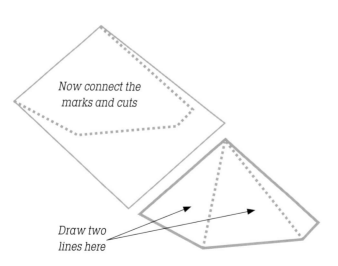

Now connect the marks and cuts

Draw two lines here

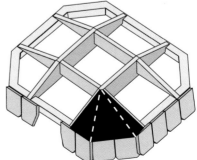

The head of my Buddha is a slightly complex, rectangular box.

The front face is a plain piece of plywood glued to the box side. I made an access panel in the back to change the light bulb or perform any maintenance. Around the top edge I fixed 2x3 pine boards with a rip cut angle. The face of the rip cut receives the upper sides of the box.

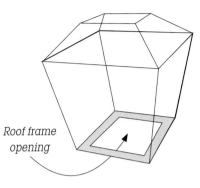

Roof frame opening

The size of the head top is not critical. So, using your eyeballs, estimate the measurement indicated by the arrow and cut a piece of plywood (A) to that height and longer than the box. Temporarily screw it to the flat surface of the 2x3.

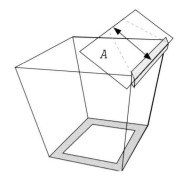

Lay a new sheet of plywood (B) on the flat surface of the next 2x3 and tuck it up under the previous sheet (A) until the edge touches; then draw a line on the underside of sheet A, indicated by dashed red line. Do the same for the other edge of A. Remove A, cut along marked lines, make a second identical piece for the other side, and glue and screw in place.

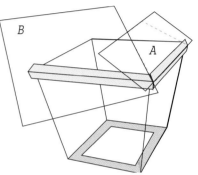

Angle cut a piece of thick plywood for the top. Glue it in place. You can now trace and cut the last two upper box pieces.

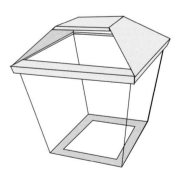

Drill four large holes in the top for illumination and cover it with clear Plexiglas.

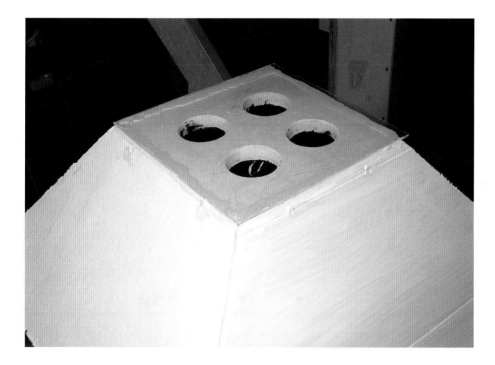

Add some 2x3 pieces on the sides to complete the helmet effect, caulk the cracks, and prime the entire head. This finishes the exterior except for the final coat of metallic gold paint.

Looking up into the head after dark.

The interior of the head is painted flat black and lined with mirrors glued to most surfaces. A hook at the top holds a small chandelier with a single 4-watt bulb.

There are seven lights on the inside. One is in the head, one under a glass dome on the main altar, and five behind large glass marbles fixed in the walls. See the electrical chapter for the particulars.

At this point the house sat finished in my basement. Over the next few weeks, I finished the platform in the maple tree that supports the new house and then moved it from my basement to its new place in the trees.

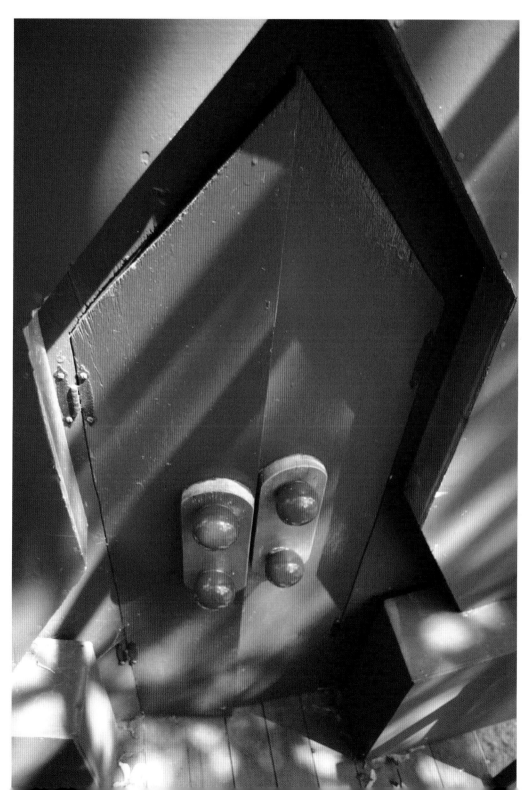

The photo on the left shows some detail of the platform and the steps. My intent was to have the platform look random and homemade with unusual steps, twists, and turns. The last picture displays the finished product ready for use.

Electrical Tips

Small lights and lanterns add much to the magic of tree houses at night. At last count there were about sixty lights here and there up in the trees, along the bridges, and in the houses. Resist the temptation to use small seasonal lights. I would love to have used strings of these lights, but they use 120 volts. Even with an isolation transformer, they have no place near little fingers.

I use the inexpensive ten-on-a-string, 4-watt, low-voltage yard lights. They are made to be rained on, frozen, wind-whipped, and safe for children and squirrels.

I put an all-weather ground fault receptacle behind some lilac bushes on the side of the house closest to the deck. I mounted the light timer and transformer next to it, where there is a large roof overhang that further keeps this hardware out of the weather. The wire from the control box runs up a pole in the bushes and from there to the solid bridge. Small staples hold the wire loosely as it is routed around the deck.

The first set of lights went up on the deck in the locust trees. I used six of the ten lights on the bridge as they came out of the box, except that I sprayed transparent color on the inside of the globes. I drilled holes in the ground stake and screwed them to the rail of the bridge. The remaining four lights were used in hanging lamps around the deck. These lamps are fairly easy to fabricate from the large variety of candle lamps sold at the garden stores.

When making lamps, I don't use the sockets that come with the yard lights; the contacts on the inexpensive sets are not that dependable. The bulbs are long-lasting, so I solder them directly on the wire. I drill a hole in the bottom or top—depending on the lamp—and secure the light with a low-temperature glue gun. The glue is easy to melt if a bulb does need to be changed.

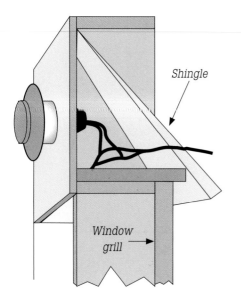

Shingle

Window grill

The next set of ten lights was installed when I finished Mary's Teahouse. Eight bulbs are inside. One is in a tube above the door on the outside and one is in a nearby lamp. Four bulbs are on the four main side panels as shown below. The original lamp is mounted sideways in a large hole; this casts indirect light on the wall. The wires are routed all around behind the shingles. Each bulb is spliced in to the main wire in parallel.

Two bulbs hang free inside the *chandelier* in the alcove in the back wall. The wire feeds in from under the shingles. Two more bulbs are in a fixture in the top center of the house. The wires simply run up the side of a rafter and into the fixture.

I used a new set of ten lights in Shadows, which brought the total to thirty lights in that area. Five lights were used around the outside base of the house. Two can be seen in the photo below, shining up on the side panels.

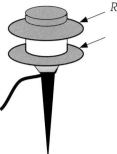

Remove these and spray the clear plastic black

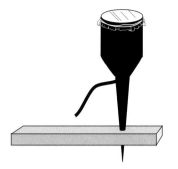

Drill a hole in a 2x4 and screw under floor of house

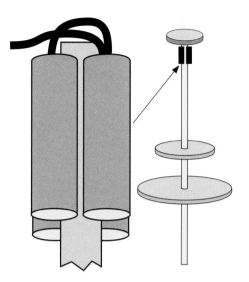

The entire fixture was used, except for the top cover and skirt. See the illustrations above.

The clear sides were spray painted black and the top covered with clear plastic wrap held in place with a rubber band.

Inside there are just four lights in tubes fixed to the top of the center pole. They shine down on the table. The last bulb is outside in a nearby lantern.

After the little church appeared in a tall pine out back, I added lights to it. There is one bulb in the bell tower and two on the altar in clear plastic globes filled with marbles. There are four bulbs on the outside over each side window. They are located behind a small plywood shape, so that the bulbs shine on the sides of the church but otherwise can't be seen from the

Interior of Shadows after dark.

ground. On the side wall beside each bulb, I drilled a large hole and cemented in a glass paperweight. This transmits diffused light to the inside. The remaining bulbs are in lanterns near the front door.

Since the church was five rope bridges away from the deck with the two houses, I decided to hang lamps at the bridge intersections and a small, tent-like room along the way. I simply made a variety of lanterns as described earlier and hung them from convenient limbs above each intersection.

In the spring of 2004, I put up the tree house called Buddha. The interior, deliberately dim, is illuminated by a chandelier in the head and by indirect lighting from the three altars. I had enough bulbs left over to hang three lanterns near the door.

This is the main altar after dark.

This is the main altar after dark.

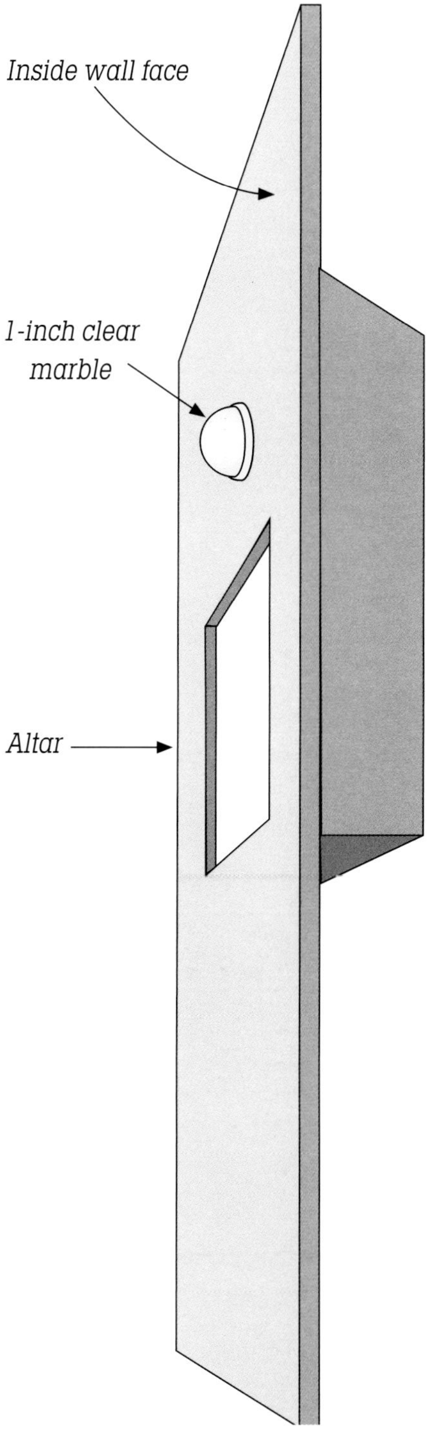

The lamps were made in the usual manner, but the glowing marbles worked so well that I will include a drawing of the design.

Drill a 1-inch hole in the wall and glue marble in place. Outline marble with gold cord or ribbon.

The position of the bulb illuminates the marble and provides indirect overhead lighting. During the day, the clear acetate provides the indirect overhead lighting. All three altars work the same.

Inside wall face

1-inch clear marble

Altar

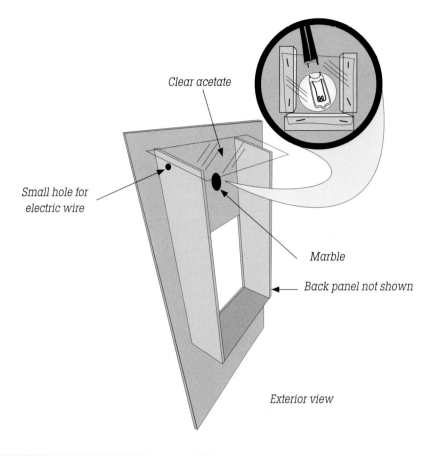

Clear acetate

Small hole for
electric wire

Marble

Back panel not shown

Exterior view

Glue and tack three small wood blocks (1-inch cross section) on back wall and staple thick clear acetate over surface as shown; this forms a pocket to drop in the bulb. These 4-watt bulbs create very little heat.

The Zip-Line

One of the most popular things in my yard is the zip-line. The line runs between two stout trees about forty-five feet apart. The launch end is about ten feet high dropping to six feet at the other end. This provides a quick (but not fast) trip. The line is kept taught during use by a come-along, which is released when not in use.

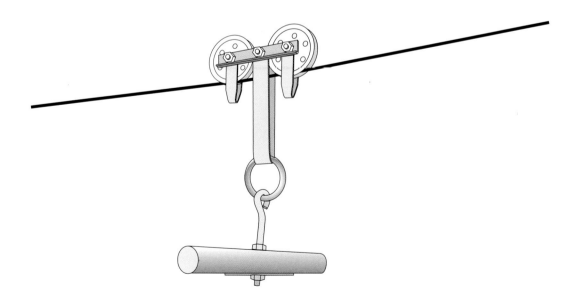

Materials list:

- Come-along
- 850 lb test aircraft cable and clamps
- Two 3-inch garage door wheels
- Length of strap steel
- Length of angle iron
- Ring and eye bolt
- 1-inch diameter wood dowel
- 1/4-inch bolt and nut

I purchased all of the materials to make a my zip-line at my local hardware store.

Below is a picture of the come-along device that I use to tighten the zip-line. Do not over tighten. Keep the cable slack when not in use.

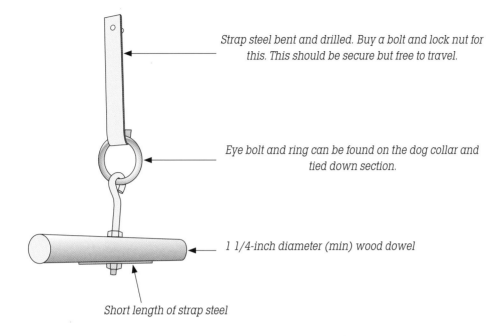

Strap steel bent and drilled. Buy a bolt and lock nut for this. This should be secure but free to travel.

Eye bolt and ring can be found on the dog collar and tied down section.

1 1/4-inch diameter (min) wood dowel

Short length of strap steel

Take two lengths of angle iron (length is not critical). Clamp together and drill three holes. Holes should be large enough to accept the wheel and center swivel bolts.

Wheels come packaged with wheel, guide, bolt, and nut (buy two packages).

Decorative Elements

Once you have a finished tree house (or two) and
a bridge (or few), it's time to add some nifty stuff.
Could be a mysterious object or a box of seashells or a
rope elevator to lift a bottle of soda up into the trees.
Sometimes it is something so strange that no one knows
what it is. If I am asked about these things, I say, "You
can have one of two things. You can have mystery and
magic or you can have answers. You can't have both.
If you have an answer, the magic and the mystery fade
away." I think this is very true. Think about it.

Epilogue

In recent years, the word ephemeral has crept more and more into my vocabulary. Our health is fine, the weather is warm, and our family prospers in every respect. We have been blessed, but the trees grow and wood planks turn from brown to gray.

There is no sadness in that observation, just an acknowledgement that life goes on, as it should. The houses still exist, and children young and old still stop by. Our objective from the beginning was to maintain our little village for as long as possible. So far, so good.

Retirement has not been what Marie and I envisioned. It has been ever so much better for both of us. For over a decade now, we have welcomed visitors from near and far to our yard. We have seven guest books filled with signatures.

We both agree that it's nice to have a future with an open end.

So, until we meet again,

Happy Trails

The author and his tolerant wife, the former Marie Kleinhenz of Louisville, Kentucky.

The author and his first bridge, built very long ago in a jungle very far away. In the photo on the right are of some of his first customers. Truth is, they were not exactly having fun.

Afterword

*What is important and significant is how
one reacts to the unexpected.*

Near the end of this book, I voice my concerns about the passage of time and the possibility that my tree house village may not survive much longer because of my age and other factors. In truth, the little houses have deteriorated for the past couple of years, as it became more difficult and dangerous for me to climb ladders. A few weeks after I wrote the Epilogue, something unexpected happened.

Here is the good news: My tree houses have been saved and will live on for many more years.

I live in a southern suburb of Rochester. My hometown is just a few miles farther south in the village of Geneseo. I have a friend who lives there—a friend with several distinct advantages. He is less than half my age, is financially secure, has a substantial property just outside of town, and has a grove of mature black walnut trees with his own tree house creations. (His tree house complex features a castle, an aerial deck, and an antique car that one may sit in.)

This past fall I made a deal with him to preserve my tree house village for the future enjoyment of children. He sent heavy equipment and a crew to take down each of the houses in one piece. The houses are now in a large, heated barn on his property.

Over the winter, he and a crew of sixty student volunteers from SUNY Geneseo will completely refurbish the houses. This spring he will begin to incorporate my houses into his facility—all connected by bridges.

Best of all—he will continue my policy of welcoming visitors, especially children.

So, I can't say, "The End." I can only say that this is the next chapter.

However, I can say once more, "Happy Trails."

—Maurice Barkley, January 2013

After the Afterword

*Life is short, so any happiness you can spread
should be done without haste.*

Hello. My name is Joseph Ferrero. Tree Creations was inspired by Maurice and Marie Barkley of Henrietta, NY. A visit while in college made me think, "This would be nice to have for my grandchildren one day," and the thought was filed away.

In May of 2011, a freak accident took the eyesight from my left eye, and, if circumstances were just slightly different, I might not be here today. This experience helped me realize the true meaning of "carpe diem" and that I may not be here for my grandchildren.

Since every man's daughter is a princess, when my girls asked for a tree house, I got to work on a castle for them. The first tree house was started on January 24, 2012—the Margrose Castle. With a deck size of almost 120 square feet, it was to be grand in every way.

During construction of this castle, we took a trip to the Long Island Children's Museum. At the museum, some automotive parts were used in creating a make-believe automobile that was enjoyed by all who touched it. Jokingly, I said to my wife, "We should put a Pinto in the tree," and then in an "ah-hah" moment, my wife and I said

"The Triumph!" In February 2012, a 1946 Triumph Renown was dragged out from my scrap pile and we started to breathe new life into it.

The Car de Triumph and the Margrose Castle were being built simultaneously and with a single purpose—to entertain children. With thoughts of tree houses in my head, I immediately remembered Maurice and Marie Barkley and their tree house village. Mr. and Mrs. Barkley had mentioned that maintenance on the tree houses was getting to be quite intensive. After some discussion, they made a decision to donate their Mystrees tree house village to the Tree Creations complex, which made for a very exciting day for my family.

Some of the tree houses from Mr. Barkley have, unfortunately, deteriorated too much to be repaired, so completely new construction will be necessary.

Although some of our construction techniques and styles are different, any reconstruction will attempt to capture the spirit of Mr. Barkley and the Mystrees magic that initially inspired me.

This is a great way to build a legacy for me and also a way to honor a man that sparks imagination. As an engineer, I have patents and trade secrets, but that part of my life will be filed away with no one to remember it. Here in Geneseo, though, the community will not soon forget Tree Creations—and the family that put a car in a tree!

Some projects presently in the works include refurbishing Maurice Barkley's tree houses, completing a village square (over 250 square feet in size) with retractable entrance stairs and an elevator to assist those that are "ground-bound" to reach the trees, and swings of various types. Plans for future projects include a small merry-go-round, a pirate ship (where, when you walk the plank, you connect to a zip-line and are launched out into the yard), a World War I style bi-plane, and a Galilean-themed observatory complete with a telescope. Please follow along with our progress on Facebook at "Tree Creations in Geneseo" or at www.TreeCreations.org. Or better yet . . . pay us a visit!

—Joseph Ferrero, January 2013

Resources

Construction Tips

The Family Handyman Tree House Building Tips
http://www.familyhandyman.com/DIY-Projects/Outdoor-Projects/Backyard-Structures
Sheds/tree-house—building-tips/View-All

Out'n'About Treehouse Construction
http://www.treehouses.com/treehouse/construction/home.html

DIY Network Double-Decker Playhouse Plans
http://www.diynetwork.com/how-to/how-to-build-a-double-decker-playhouse/index.html

Popular Mechanics How to Build a Backyard Tree House
http://www.popularmechanics.com/home/how-to-plans/woodworking/4350648

The Red Beacon Ultimate Tree House Building Guide
http://www.redbeacon.com/hg/ultimate-tree-house-building-guide/

Self Build Tree House and Deck Plans for Beginners
http://treehouseguides.com/

Tree House by Design
http://treehousebydesign.com/

The Treehouse Guide
http://www.thetreehouseguide.com/building.htm

Tree House Supplies

American Arborist Supplies
http://www.arborist.com/

Nelson Treehouse and Supply
http://www.nelsontreehousesupply.com/plans.html

TreehouseSupplies.com
http://www.treehousesupplies.com/

Great Ideas to Inspire You

Blue Forest Tree House Design & Construction
http://www.blueforest.com/bespoke-treehouses#.UQGhxB12xnQ

Custom Tree House Plans
http://dornob.com/custom-tree-house-plans-diy-ideas-building-designs/

The Treehouse Guys
http://www.treehouses.org/

In-Person Workshops

TreeHouse Workshop
http://www.treehouseworkshop.com/

List of Tree House Conferences
http://www.treehouses.com/treehouse/construction/workshops.html

The TreeHouse Workshop of Seattle
http://www.treehugger.com/sustainable-product-design/the-treehouse-workshop-of-seattle.html

Tree Top Builders Workshop
http://www.treetopbuilders.net/tree-house-workshops.htm

Index

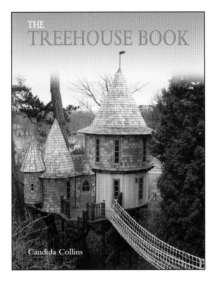

The Treehouse Book
by Candida Collins

Tree houses have come of age. The image of a few planks nailed into the branches of a tree has changed into a new generation of specially designed and built structures, suitable as playhouses, studies, or even guestrooms. Totally inhabitable and filled with designer furniture, plumbing, and electronic wizardry, the twenty tree houses featured in this book are to be admired, dreamed about, and even built.

Featuring spectacular photography of exteriors set up among the trees, and interior shots that offer design ideas for living the "high" life, *The Treehouse Book* offers a fairy tale castle, a thatched cottage, a complete hotel, and much more. Each project was designed using computer technology and built using sustainable materials to create structures that only seem like fantasy. Each is cleverly fitted to the chosen trees, avoiding long-term damage to these remarkable structures.

$19.95 Hardcover • ISBN 978-1-60239-761-3

ALSO AVAILABLE

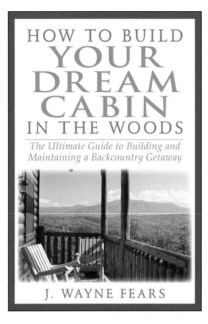

How to Build Your Dream Cabin in the Woods
The Ultimate Guide to Building and Maintaining a Backcountry Getaway
by J. Wayne Fears

Here is the ultimate resource for finally turning your dream into reality. With photos, blueprints, and diagrams, Fears thoroughly covers the process of constructing the cabin you've always wanted. Covering topics like buying land, construction materials, deciding on lighting, the water system, and on-site constructions—such as shooting ranges, an outhouse, or an outside fire ring—this is a book filled with nuggets of wisdom from a specialist in the field. J. Wayne Fears is a wildlife biologist by training who has organized big game hunting camps, guided canoe trips, and run commercial getaway operations. He built his own log cabin in the early 1990s and has been enjoying it ever since. Now you can build and enjoy the cabin you've always dreamed of, too.

$12.95 Paperback • ISBN 978-1-61608-041-9

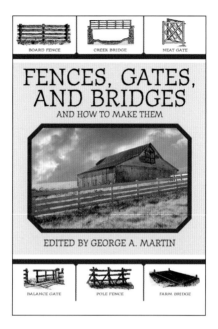

Fences, Gates, and Bridges
And How to Make Them

Edited by George A. Martin

First published in 1887, *Fences, Gates, and Bridges* is an instructional guide to the best ways to build a variety of fences, gates, hedges, bridges, and culverts. The section on fences boasts a wealth of information on building various types of fences, including rail, composite, garden, board, and picket. It also explores how to construct an effective barbed wire fence, explains how to use a stone wall to reinforce a wooden fence, and highlights the pros of building portable fences. *Fences, Gates, and Bridges* is a classic manual for anyone who wants to build their own structures for their farm, large property, or quaint backyard.

$9.95 Paperback • ISBN 978-1-61608-129-4

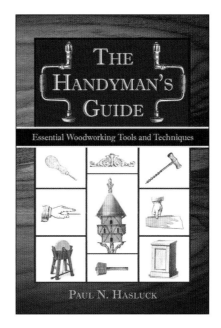

The Handyman's Guide

Essential Woodworking Tools and Techniques

by Paul N. Hasluck

This comprehensive guide to the tools and techniques of woodworking has been a favorite of both amateur and professional woodworkers for over a century. Readers will learn to make almost anything using only hand tools. With nearly three thousand illustrations, this definitive guide is an invaluable resource for any do-it-yourselfer.

From identifying and holding tools properly to constructing your own household furniture, *The Handyman's Guide* is your trusted resource for all things related to woodwork. Precise illustrations and design details provide a map for hundreds of woodworking projects, including gates, sheds, trellises, tables, yard and garden accessories, fences, porches, furniture, cabinets, and much more. If it's wood, and there's work to be done, don't start without Paul N. Hasluck's essential guide.

$12.95 Paperback • ISBN 978-1-62039-173-4